OLD MEMORIES

OLD MEMORIES

BY

GENERAL SIR HUGH GOUGH

G.C.B., V.C.

GYAN

Published by

Gyan Publishing House
5, Ansari Road
Daryaganj, New Delhi-110002
Phone: 011-47034999, 9811692060
E-mail: books@gyanbooks.com

Distribution Network
gyanbooks.com
India, USA, Canada, UK, Australia, France

ISBN: 978-81-212-7773-0 (PB)
First Published, 1897

2nd Impression 2023

Printed at: Gyan Press, Delhi.

OLD MEMORIES
Author: HUGH GOUGH

OLD MEMORIES

OLD MEMORIES

BY

GENERAL SIR HUGH GOUGH

G.C.B., V.C.

WILLIAM BLACKWOOD AND SONS
EDINBURGH AND LONDON
MDCCCXCVII

CONTENTS.

I.

II.

OLD MEMORIES.

I.

I PROPOSE writing from memory, and with the aid of some old letters written during the time of the Mutiny and later, such portions of my military career as may possibly be interesting to my friends and family.

I was gazetted cornet in the 3rd Light Cavalry on September 4th, 1853, and joined my regiment at Meerut shortly after. The 3rd Light Cavalry was then considered one of the best of the ten regiments of regular cavalry in the East India Company's service. At the time of which I write the Company's Bengal army consisted of regular and irregular troops. There were ten regiments of regular or light cavalry, and seventy-four regiments of regular infantry. These regiments were all armed, dressed, and disciplined, as well as officered, exactly on the same lines as the British troops—a fact which would seem very strange and incongruous to the military eye of the present day, more especially to those who see the Bengal Cavalry as they now are—when dress and efficiency are made to combine, and the imitation dragoon is carefully avoided.

For instance, in the days before the

Mutiny we were mounted on horses the property of Government, the men dressed in dragoon costume, officered by a full complement of British officers, and drilled to perfection as "dragoons." In the 3rd Light Cavalry we used to pride ourselves on being steadier on parade than the British cavalry regiment then stationed at Meerut; and proud we were of the old regiment.

Our commanding officer was Lieutenant-Colonel G. Carmichael Smyth; our adjutant, Lieutenant Sanford, afterwards a most brilliant *sabreur* in the Mutiny, who lost his life at the siege of Lucknow under very sad circumstances.

Meerut was garrisoned by one regiment of British cavalry, one of native light cavalry, one regiment of British and two of native infantry, with the headquarters of the Bengal Artillery, and some two or three batteries, horse and field. It was one of the pleasantest and most favourite stations in the Bengal Presidency. There was a great deal of sport and gaiety, which all subalterns like, and I confess I took my full share of both. The regiments in the garrison were singularly sociable; and in the midst of fun and gaiety, which was to most of us the apparent object of life, there was little thought or apprehension of anything so serious as war breaking out. The Punjab had been completely pacified, our frontiers appeared unusually quiet, and, seeing all things the same around us, our martial spirit distinctly lay low.

Such was our life up to the spring of 1857. In the early part of that year vague rumours began to be spread as to the disinclination of the sepoys to accept a new pattern cartridge which Government had ordered to be issued. One or two camps of musketry instruction had been formed, for the education of detachments from native infantry regiments in the use of the new rifle about to be introduced, in lieu of the old Brown Bess. In these camps there had been some grumbling and discontent evinced, but I believe no actual insubordination. After a time the discontent spread, and so strongly evinced itself in two native infantry regiments stationed down country that one corps mutinied against its officers, and was disbanded, the men returning to their homes and spreading discontent and sedition in every station through which they passed. The other regiment being also disarmed and the men sent to their homes, in like manner spread the flames of sedition. I myself, about this period, had gone on leave to Cawnpore and Lucknow, and it was evident in both of these places that all was not right. Houses were burnt, the men were sulky and insubordinate, and other signs were apparent; but such was our fatal belief in our security that no amount of warnings alarmed us. At Cawnpore I remember well seeing the notorious Nana Sahib driving about, and hearing on all sides of his attention and hospitality to Europeans. Little did I then think that ere long he would be the leader of the bloody massacre at Cawnpore, wherein perished so many of my old friends and comrades (among them the dearest friend I had in the world), or that in less than a year after I should be in hot pursuit of him personally, and (I regret to say) only just miss catching him.

After the disbandment and disarmament of the two regiments of native infantry matters seemed to smooth down, though it is evident, from after-knowledge, that a very widespread conspiracy was being hatched.

It was about this time that the mysterious circulation of chupatties throughout the country took place—from village to village and from town to town—causing a general wonder and attracting the notice of the newspapers and civil authorities,—though the portent was not deemed by any means so serious as it was, and I believe to this day the real meaning has never been clearly explained.

In those days of rather easy soldiering it was usual to open the leave season on April 15th, and suspend all further parades (excepting adjutants' drills and company or troop parades) for the hot weather. This probably had been the custom from time immemorial: hitherto our campaigns had all been fought in the cold weather, friends and foes alike preferring to avoid the unpleasantness of exposure and fighting in the extreme heat of the summer months. Whether it was part of the plan of conspiracy to bring on events, however, during the season when Europeans were supposed to be unable to cope with the climate, I cannot say. It might have been mere chance. At any rate, the Mutiny was precipitated in a manner which took the whole kingdom by surprise, and launched us in a war for which we were totally unprepared, and at a season when the perils from climate were far greater than from any visible enemy.

I may here explain that hitherto it had been customary to bite off the end of the cartridge, before loading the carbine, in order to loosen the powder. The objection raised by the sepoys to the new cartridges was, that Government had caused them to be lubricated with fat, the contact of which with their teeth would deprive them of their caste. Moreover, the stirrers-up of sedition had persuaded the men that it was the intention of the British Government, by smearing the cartridges with pig's or cow's fat, not only to cause them to lose caste, but to forcibly convert them to Christianity. This idea might well gain credence amongst these ignorant followers of the Mohammedan religion, which itself had been formed on coercive principles: at all events the idea became general, and caused universal consternation. With a view to remove these suspicions on the part of the men, our commanding officer, Colonel Carmichael Smyth, ordered a parade of the skirmishers (fifteen men per troop only being armed with carbines were so designated) in order to explain to them that, as they were not required to bite off the end of the cartridge, but merely to tear it off with their fingers, there could be no prejudice to their caste. The parade took place about the beginning of May, when Colonel Smyth explained to the men the new mode of handling the cartridges. To his utter surprise and consternation, of the ninety men present, only five would even accept the cartridges served out to them, although they were aware they were the old ones taken out of the magazine. The remaining eighty-five men absolutely refused to touch them, or to obey the commanding officer's orders. The men were respectful, but most decided in their refusal. The colonel and his officiating adjutant, Lieutenant Melville Clarke, were helpless, and the parade was dismissed. There was but one course to follow—to report the matter to the General, and through him to army headquarters. This being done, an order promptly returned ordering the whole body to be tried by court-martial.

They were forthwith placed in confinement in an old hospital building near their lines, and under a guard of a company of the 60th Rifles. From that date premonitory signs of impending sedition showed themselves in Meerut; one or two bungalows and some huts in the men's lines were burnt down, and there were unheeded tokens of an ill feeling among the natives in the bazaars, &c.; but as there was no overt act of insubordination, and no attempt whatever to rescue the prisoners, the authorities never dreamt of any resistance to the orders of Government, whatever they might be. Under these circumstances of fancied security and quiet the general court-martial on the eighty-five prisoners of the 3rd Light Cavalry took place. The court was composed entirely of native officers, some from the regiments at Meerut, and some from the native garrison at Delhi. It was assisted by one

British officer, under the title of "Superintending officer," whose advice and legal knowledge probably considerably influenced their opinions. This court-martial, held in the large mess-room of the British cavalry regiment, was a strange sight to witness, and I, with many others equally interested, was an anxious observer. The president and members of the court, together with the Superintending officer, were all seated at the mess-table whilst the prisoners were paraded for trial.

After their first arraignment, all pleading "not guilty," they were allowed to sit down on the ground. It was curious to watch their faces — some, especially the older soldiers, men who had seen and done good service, and wore several medals, looking worn and anxious; others looking sullen and apparently unconcerned, and, native-like, trusting to fate. The proceedings were not long. After the usual forms of procedure, the colonel, the adjutant, and the havildar major gave their evidence. In no case did any of the prisoners attempt any cross-examination, and the only incident which occurred was during the evidence of the acting adjutant, Lieutenant Melville Clarke, when some of them stood up, rather excitedly crying, "Did the Adjutant Sahib say that?" and, on the evidence being repeated, adding loudly, "It's a lie, it's a lie!"

When the proceedings were concluded, the men were marched back to their place of confinement in the old hospital, still guarded by the 60th Rifles; and the proceedings and sentences were at once

GENERAL THE HON. GEORGE ANSON.

(*After Count d'Orsay.*)

sent up to army headquarters for the Commander-in-Chief's approval.

The Commander-in-Chief at that time was General the Honourable George Anson. He had previously commanded the Meerut Division, and the 3d Light Cavalry had been then under his command. He was a very popular man as a divisional commander, pleasant and agreeable to all, and I personally had met with great kindness from him. It must have been a severe trial to find himself placed at such a time in a position of so great responsibility, and one where experience, nerve, and decision were so much needed —indeed, a position that few men could face with confidence and self-trust. His successor in the command of the Meerut Division was General Hewitt, an old man who had seen and done good service, but whose years and infirmities would in these days have disqualified him for such a command. But to return to the court-martial: the proceedings having been submitted to the Commander-in-Chief for approval, and the confirmation having been received by telegram on Friday, May 8, a general parade of the troops quartered at Meerut was ordered for the next day, Saturday, the 9th. The parade took place at an early hour that morning, and there were present, the general officer commanding the Meerut Division (Major-General Hewitt) and his staff, Brigadier Archdale Wilson commanding at Meerut, and the following troops: two battteries of Bengal Artillery, 6th Dragoon Guards (the Carabiniers), the 60th Rifles, 3rd Light Cavalry, 11th and 20th Native

Infantry. The troops were formed in three sides of a square, the European troops forming two sides, and I believe I am right in saying all prepared for action if necessary; the native troops had their firearms but no ball ammunition, and our regiment was dismounted.

The proceedings and sentences of the court-martial were then read out, the prisoners being in the centre of the square. The sentences on the prisoners varied according to their length of service: the older soldiers were sentenced to transportation or imprisonment for life, the remainder for fifteen, twenty, and ten years, but none less than ten years. They were then fettered in front of the troops, and were marched away to the civil gaol. As they passed our regiment, carrying their boots, which had been taken off for the purpose of fixing the fetters (which were simply leg-irons), a number of them threw them at the Colonel, cursing him loudly in Hindustani, and calling to their comrades to remember them. There was a good deal of murmuring in our ranks, and had it not been for the presence of the British troops it is impossible to say what might not have taken place. The parade was dismissed, and we marched our men back to their lines on foot. Nothing occurred on the way, and it seemed as if the men accepted the situation as inevitable: they were perfectly quiet when dismissed, and there was nothing to show how angry they felt at the punishment meted out to their comrades, most of whom were men of long service, and had many relations in the regiment. As a matter of fact, the "skirmishers" of the regiment were more or less picked men, and quite the *élite* of the corps. The sad business of the morning being over, we returned to our various daily occupations, little thinking what stern realities of life would so shortly be rudely thrust upon us. On the afternoon of the same day officers commanding the troops to which the prisoners had belonged went to the civil gaol to settle the men's accounts of pay, &c. Shall I ever forget the scene? It made the strongest impression on me, though I was but a thoughtless young subaltern. We found our men imprisoned in one large ward: at first they seemed sullen or impassive, until it entered their comprehensions that it was all a sad reality, that they were now being paid up and discharged from an honourable service, into which as it were they had been born; for in those days the career of a soldier descended from father to son, and men were born into their profession —a profession which in the good old days of John Company was considered the most honourable a man could belong to; soldiers were held in the highest esteem in their villages, had prior legal rights to any others, and were looked up to by all. Now, alas! this good professional reputation is an idea of the past, and no longer does the native soldier's profession rank amongst his compeers as *the* one of all, or descend as a matter of course to his son. We have wiped out all this in our many reforms.

But to return to our men. Once they began to realise all they were losing, and the terrible future before them, they broke down completely. Old soldiers, with many medals gained in desperately-fought battles for their English masters, wept bitterly, lamenting their sad fate, and imploring their officers to save them from their future; young soldiers, too, joined in, and I have seldom, if ever, in all my life, experienced a more touching scene. To me, a young soldier of barely four years' service, it came with the deepest effect, and I believe I was weak enough almost to share their sorrow. It was very evident they, at any rate, knew but little of the events that would follow —as indeed did any of us. That very evening a native officer of my troop came to me, under pretence of making up the accounts. After a time he made the following report: that a mutiny of the native troops at Meerut would certainly take place the next day, Sunday, May 10th, further stating that the Native Infantry were going to rise, that the 3rd Cavalry would also do so, and that they intended to release their comrades in gaol. The native officer belonged to my own troop, but as I was only in temporary command I did not know him very well, and to this day I have never been able to understand why he should have come to me. Still there was the fact, and on the strength of it I went at once to my colonel and told him what had been secretly reported to me. He treated the communication with contempt, reproving me for listening to such idle words. I met the brigadier that evening, and told him the same story, but he also was incredulous. Such was our ill-judged confidence! But, indeed, few men would in those days have been inclined to believe in the "treachery" of our native soldiers.

The next day was the ever-memorable 10th of May—Sunday. In the early morning I drove to church with young Macnabb of my regiment, a very fine young fellow who had lately joined us, full of bright youth and vigour. How well I remember that Sunday morning—even to noticing Macnabb's frock-coat! We were in undress summer uniform, frock-coats and white overalls, the former made of some very light material. Macnabb's was of alpaca, but with the wrong lace. I drew his attention to this, telling him he must be sure to correct it or the colonel would find fault. The very noticing of this helped me afterwards to identify him. In church we sat near my friends the Greatheds. Mr Greathed was Commissioner of Meerut, a most popular man, and greatly respected by all. They had always been extremely kind to me. Mrs Greathed spoke to us after church about the events of the previous day. When we separated Macnabb left me to spend the day with some friends in the Bengal Artillery. It was the last time I ever saw him alive. The day for me was passed as many a careless youngster even now spends the long hot-weather Sunday (for in the middle of May the days are both long and hot). I had many ponies to look after, both of my own and my chum Sanford's; and I had several tame pets, amongst them two bears and a leopard: one bear, however, had lately become too savage to be much of a playfellow, and I had been obliged to shoot him, so I amused myself with the other. About five o'clock in the afternoon, whilst dressing for duty (I was orderly officer that day), my servants came running in with the alarming intelligence that the Native Infantry lines were on fire, and bungalows were being burnt; and immediately after a native officer with two orderlies galloped up, calling loudly for "the Sahib." I rushed out, half dressed, and at once recognised the native officer who had visited me the evening before. He was greatly excited, and called on me to mount my horse and accompany him—stating that the Native Infantry were in open mutiny and were murdering their officers, and that our regiment was arming and mounting. The fact was very apparent that something terrible had occurred, as volleys of musketry could be heard from the Native Infantry lines, and clouds of smoke from houses all around blazing up told the tale of destruction which had begun. My charger, a very fine black (half Arab, half Waler), had been already ordered, and the syce came running up to me with him. A most singular incident here occurred. Hitherto this horse had always shown the utmost disinclination to let me mount: he was very nervous and vicious, and I could never get on him without much coaxing and delay. On this occasion, as the syce trotted him up to me holding a bunch of lucerne grass in his hand, the horse took one crunch at it, and at the same time allowed me to mount without any difficulty; and never again did I experience any further trouble with him, and he did me rare good service that night and for many a day after, till he succumbed to hard work before Delhi.

As soon as I was mounted I determined to see for myself what was the real state of affairs at the Native Infantry lines, much against the wishes of my escort, who, however, accompanied me. I galloped down by the parade-ground of the 20th Native Infantry, avoiding the lines, where I should inevitably have been murdered. When within view of them I saw a sight which has been indelibly stamped on my memory. These lines, usually a scene of perfect discipline and neatness, with rows of mud barracks neatly thatched, with the quarter-guard ready to turn out, and with groups of well-dressed and happy contented sepoys lounging about, were now the scene of the most wild and awful confusion: the huts on fire, the sepoys (in each regiment over a thousand strong) having seized their arms and ammunition, dancing and leaping frantically about, calling and yelling to each other, and blazing away into the air and in all directions—absolutely a maddened crowd of fiends and devils, all thirsting for the blood of their officers, and of Europeans generally. I confess I was appalled at the sight, and saw at once it was no place for me: their madness had got the mastery over them, and I was in the extremest peril. The sepoys had seen me approaching with my escort, and as

I pulled up in wonder and horror, they shouted to my men to leave me, and began to rush forward, firing as they came. The native officer implored of me to turn back; and indeed it was high time, for as I turned to leave, and galloped away, a volley was fired—but fortunately without effect. I then determined to go to our own lines, for it was evident there was much stirring there too. I went straight to my own troop—the first troop according to number on the right of the lines. There I found everything in the utmost disorder: the men had thrown off all control and discipline, and were wildly excited; most of them were mounted and galloping to and fro, the lines were being burnt, and there was a general rush to the magazine, where the men helped themselves to the ammunition—regardless of its being the "unclean cartridge." As for any efforts on my part to bring them to a sense of their duties or of obedience to my orders, they were absolutely useless, and I felt myself most unmistakably *de trop!* Still no attempts were made on my life, thanks to the care taken of me by the native officers, and most especially of my individual friend and his escort. After a time, however, the disregard of my authority changed to open mutiny; there were loud shouts of "*Maro, Maro!*" ("Kill him, kill him!") and a few men, chiefly recruits, fired pistol-shots at me, mostly at random, although one shot so far took effect as to pierce the cantle of my saddle. The situation became critical:

I was alone, or rather the one Englishman there, and helpless amongst them; when just at this moment I saw the quartermaster-sergeant, by name Cunninghame, wildly galloping up, pursued by several troopers with drawn swords. Seeing me he flew to my side; and now my men, being joined by these open mutineers, who were bent on murdering him, also broke into undisguised mutiny. Seeing all was lost, and that my power as their officer was absolutely gone, and acting on the earnest, in fact forcible, solicitation of the better disposed (for they took my horse's head and forced me to leave), we decided to make the best of our way to the European lines. We left at a gallop, being for a time pursued with shouts and execrations; though I do not even now believe that the wish of the men was to take our lives or prevent our escape, for had it been so we could not have got away.

Thus was my farewell taken of my troop and the regiment of which I had always felt so proud. It was a desperate moment, and my feelings of grief and despair at the turn events had taken I can well remember. But time did not then admit of any regrets or thoughts, save of personal safety. Though no longer pursued by our men, Cunninghame and I had to force our way through the only road open to us, and this was the native bazaar, which—such was the singularly unanimous outbreak of fanatical and race feeling—was up in arms; the roads were crowded with foes, and we had literally to cut our way, pelted with stones, through hundreds of men, armed with tulwars and *lathies* (iron-bound cudgels). But our speed saved us, and we got through safely, though bruised and beaten. In these days of quiet India, one can hardly realise the very hell of fury and hatred through which we passed—men who had hitherto always salaamed to almost all Europeans now thirsting for their blood! Having charged safely through the throng, my first impulse was to gallop to the rescue of Mr and Mrs Greathed. They lived in a large house in the civil lines, beyond the cantonment—on the other side of the bazaar, where of course they would have been exposed to the great fury of the bazaar people. In fact, I could see they were even then on their way to the house, and as we entered the gates there were men close behind us. I galloped up to the door, and there was met by the Commissioner's servants, all evidently aware of the disturbance that was going on in the neighbouring bazaar. They all knew me well, and at once greeted me with the welcome intelligence that their master and mistress had already made their escape and had driven away. They were naturally excited, but it was only afterwards I recalled to mind what had not struck me at the time—viz., their evident wish for my departure, assuring me over and over again that Mr and Mrs Greathed were safe. Having no further object in remaining, and seeing the rapid approach of the rioters, I turned my horse and galloped off in the direction of the European lines.

And here I must relate what was actually the case: the faithful servants, knowing how short the time was, and the improbability of their being able to get the carriage ready to convey away their master and mistress, to whom they were devotedly and faithfully attached, had persuaded Mr Greathed and his wife to take refuge on the top of the house—a very large flat-roofed bungalow—and were themselves assembled at the door, in order to assure the mob, whose immediate advent was such a certainty, that their intended victims had escaped. And so it happened: I had scarcely departed when the crowd arrived, loudly calling on the servants to bring out the Commissioner, on whose death they were bent. I leave to imagination the feelings of my friends, when from the roof of their house they saw me, whom they recognised, galloping up to the house, and, after a brief parley, taking an equally speedy departure. For a second their thoughts dwelt on the possible treachery of their servants, and seeing the compound being rapidly invaded by the miscreants from the bazaar, their hearts failed them, and death seemed to stare them in the face. Some of the servants, however, speedily reassured them, and, pointing out the utter impossibility of an escape in the face of the rapid approach of their enemies, again and again vowed that they would save them. In the meantime the house was broken into by the maddened crowd, who, robbed of their prey, revenged themselves by a thorough looting of the premises—a general smash of everything; and finally, setting fire to the house, departed bent on fresh plunder and hopes of massacre. On their departure the servants persuaded Mr and Mrs Greathed to descend from the roof of the burning house, and secreted them in the garden; and most fortunately so, for not long afterwards a number of the people returned, having somehow heard that the Commissioner was still about the place, and they then not only searched the premises but also the garden — happily without success. The anxiety of both master and servants may be imagined whilst the search was being made, and until their would-be murderers finally retreated. I believe the final escape was made next morning.

After leaving the Greatheds' house I

made my way, still escorted by my loyal native officer and his two sowars, to the Artillery lines, where, having brought me in safety, they made their final salute and left me, notwithstanding my earnest entreaties and persuasions that they should remain with me,—the native officer averring that his duty was with his regimental comrades, and whether for life or death they must return to the regiment. And so we parted, after several hours of the most anxious and trying dangers; and for ever — for, notwithstanding all my efforts, I never heard again of my friend the native officer. I knew his name, of course; but though I found out his house, in the Oude District, no trace of him was ever again found, and I could only conclude he met his death at Delhi in the mutineers' camp. A braver or more loyal man I have never met, and, whatever his faults may have subsequently been, in his mutiny against his salt and his military allegiance, all will allow his loyalty to me was beyond praise, and I can never forget him, or how he risked his life again and again to save mine.

But this was by no means a solitary instance of the personal loyalty of our men to their officers. Both Captain Craigie and Lieutenant Mackenzie, with their families, were guarded by their own men and brought out in safety. Indeed I may say that not a single officer's life was taken by our own men, though subsequently at Delhi they were the chief leaders in the massacre which occurred at that place.

II.

HAVING thus made my way safely into the lines of the Bengal Artillery, I found the whole place in an extreme ferment—every one in the greatest anxiety as to what had really occurred, numbers of refugees from the native lines and bazaars having brought in ghastly accounts of the burning of houses and massacre of Europeans, &c. Night was partially setting in, and, strange to say, not a movement had as yet been made for either succour or vengeance. There appeared to be a general paralysis. General Hewitt was, as I said before, a very old officer, and on this occasion was completely unmanned. He had more or less relegated his authority to Brigadier Archdale Wilson, the commandant of artillery and next senior officer. The British troops consisted of Tombs' Troop of Horse Artillery (one of the finest batteries of that magnificent arm), a battery of field artillery, the 6th Dragoon Guards (the Carabiniers), and the first battalion of the 60th Rifles. The Carabiniers had recently arrived in India, and—with the exception of one squadron, called the Crimean Squadron, consisting of old soldiers who had served in the Russian campaign—was composed of young and almost raw recruits; their horses were remounts, and only partially trained; so that the regiment could scarcely be called thoroughly efficient. I would, however, bear record to the magnificent services performed by the Carabiniers during the rest of the campaign—especially at Delhi, and in the North-West Provinces and Rohilkund. On a Sunday evening, when there was not the least expectation of such an *émeute*, or of any disturbance, the troops were naturally more unprepared than on any ordinary week-day. Indeed it was said, and I believe on good foundation, that it was the original intention of the mutineers to attack the British lines that evening, hoping to find the troops attending church without their firearms, which was the custom in those days.

On my arrival I learnt it had just been decided to move the troops, who were all assembled ready, through the native lines to disperse the mutineers. Alas! too late! Time had been wasted; the opportunity was lost; and as we advanced it became more and more evident the mutineers had made good their escape, and it was equally evident they had gone in scattered bodies to the royal city of Delhi, there to lead to further mutiny and raise the general revolt in favour of the King of Delhi.

It was stated that Major Rosser of the Carabiniers—a fine, gallant soldier, afterwards killed at the assault of Delhi—had earnestly implored the brigadier to allow him to take his squadron and a couple of horse-artillery guns and pursue the mutineers—even to the walls of Delhi. This gallant offer was not accepted. It is not for me to criticise the reasons why; but I have always felt firmly convinced that, had it been carried out, Delhi would have been saved. Even if the 3rd Light Cavalry mutineers had arrived before the pursuing force, I believe the moral effect of the approach of the British troopers would have deterred the Native Infantry troops from breaking out, and Delhi would have been saved. This is still my opinion after many years' service, when time after time I have seen the wonderful effect of dash and promptitude, especially on the native mind. But to return to our own immediate movements.

The British troops slowly advanced, with every precaution, through the native lines, which were empty and in flames; the guns fired a few rounds into a tope of trees said to be occupied, but which was as empty as the lines, and returned through the bazaar and the cantonments lately occupied by the officers of the native regiments, did nothing, saw nothing, and found nothing, except the sad relics of the late evening's outbreak in the shape of mutilated remains of their fellow-countrymen and women. It was here my sad experience to discover and identify the remains of my brother-officer young Macnabb, from whom I parted that Sunday morning at the church door, now lying on the road dead. Had it not been for his great height and the peculiar braid on his frock-coat, on which I had remarked in the morning, I should not have been able to identify him. Happily I had reason to believe his death must have been instantaneous. I afterwards heard that he had been spending the day with some friends in the artillery lines, and, hearing the disturbance, borrowed a horse from an officer in the artillery, and galloped off to his duty with his regiment, meeting his death on the way.

I have alluded to the peculiar dislike of my horse to being mounted. It is a curious fact that when, for the first time that night, I dismounted in order to identify Macnabb's body, he then allowed me to remount without the slightest demur, and never afterwards played his old tricks.

The morning after the mutiny a small force of cavalry and horse artillery went out and made a sort of pursuit down the road to Delhi; but, as a matter of course, nothing was to be seen. I accompanied the force, and was attached to the Carabiniers temporarily. On our return I took the opportunity to visit my house, in order to see what damage had been done and if anything was recoverable. Alas! *everything* was destroyed, nothing had been saved, and my house was but a mass of smouldering ruins. My servants—notably my factotum, Madar Bux, otherwise known as "Mr Bux," one of the very best and most trustworthy native servants I have ever met—had all remained faithful. He (Mr Bux), in his anxiety to save what he considered most valuable, had managed to secure my full-dress uniform—a very costly and gorgeous costume of French-grey and silver, hussar pattern (but which from that moment was of no more use to me than as a fancy dress, as the uniform was subsequently discarded)—neglecting, alas! to secure anything else that would have been precious and useful to me. I was thus left stranded with the summer uniform in which I had escaped, the full-dress clothes he had saved, and nothing else in the wide world — a good start for a campaign which lasted for so many long months through summer and winter!

Fortunately my syces also, with one exception, had remained faithful, and had guarded my horses. I had recently bought a valuable black Arab for racing purposes. He and his syce had disappeared. Probably some mutineer leader rode my handsome purchase at Delhi, but I never saw or heard of him again. I wish I had been as fortunate with him as I was with a cigar-case I lost that night, which, in the autumn of 1875, a Ghoorkha rifleman picked up on the roadside on the march between Almorah and Delhi, when proceeding with his battalion to the camp of exercise held there that year. He took it to his commanding officer, who, seeing in faded writing the words "Hugh Gough, Cornet, 3rd Light Cavalry, Meerut, 1854," sent the case to me, thinking it might be an old friend, as, indeed, it was. What its adventures had been since that trying day and during the eighteen years we had been parted, there was nothing but conjecture. It was a curious case of missing treasure-trove.

On our return to cantonments we found that it had been decided to concentrate all the British troops at one end of the station; and an intrenchment was already in course of erection, where the ladies, convalescents, and stores were collected, in order to be safe from attack. As the native troops had all gone to Delhi, our only enemies now were the bazaar people and the neighbouring villagers. These promptly took up arms, and, unrepressed by civil or military force, looted and fought amongst themselves. In fact, complete anarchy prevailed in and about Meerut; and, to make matters worse, on the outbreak of the 3rd Light Cavalry, their first and natural impulse had been to release their comrades in the civil gaol, which they did without opposition, and in so doing also let loose hundreds of civil offenders, gaol-birds of the worst description—murderers, thieves, and vagabonds—who were now free to wreak their wicked will without let or hindrance. Many and sad were the cases of travellers on the Grand Trunk road (the great line of communication between Calcutta and Meerut and onward into the Punjab) being robbed and murdered, and few were the escapes. I remember, however, one young officer—Lieutenant J. Robinson, who was on his way to join our regiment at Meerut—arriving a day or two after the Mutiny broke out. He had been stopped in his *dawk ghari* (travelling carriage) on the Grand Trunk road, robbed of everything he possessed, his companion murdered, whilst he, curious to say, was spared on account of his youth. But seldom was the plea, either of youth or sex, respected.

Our own losses in the regiment on the night of the Mutiny were Lieutenant Macnabb, and Veterinary Surgeons Parry and Dawson, while Surgeon - Major Christie was desperately wounded. He and another officer were attacked when driving in a buggy and attempting to escape; Dr Christie was left for dead covered with wounds, his companion being killed. The former recovered to a certain extent, but was invalided for life. As I have said, none of our officers hitherto were killed by our own men; the casualties I have mentioned were from the hands of the Native Infantry sepoys, or the bazaar *budmashes.* Our colonel, who was most unpopular, and more especially so owing to his action in the "cartridge" incident, was, however, one of the first objects of the men's vengeance: a strong party at once went to his house with the avowed intention of murdering him. But he had received timely intimation of their advent, and had made his escape. That night, with the exception of some forty or fifty men, the whole of the regiment went off to Delhi. History elsewhere tells us how they originated the mutiny and massacre there, and proved themselves such incarnate fiends—a curious contrast to their behaviour to their own officers the evening before, and one of the many instances of inexplicable mixture of loyalty and treachery in our native soldiers in this crisis.

The morning of May 11th was a sad and mournful one at Meerut, with its tale of disaster and death and separation for so many, who the day before little dreamt of the "terrible unexpected" which had overwhelmed the station. It was also a day of shame and self-contempt, as we all felt and acknowledged that nothing had been done, no attempt made to stem the wave of disaster, and that those who had brought on us this awful blow were for the present safe from our reach within the walls of Delhi—whence, too, soon came the news of the further and worse massacre, with the tidings that a new ruler had risen in India, in the newly-proclaimed King of Delhi, and that the British Raj was declared to be at an end.

I was now appointed to do duty with the Carabiniers, the officers of which regiment were most kind and hospitable; and no longer having a home of my own, I found one with them. On May 19th I was startled by hearing from a friend (Lieutenant Waterfield) that news had reached Meerut of a party of fugitives wandering about in the vicinity of Delhi. The news had been

KING OF DELHI. *(From a Native Print.)*

conveyed by a letter written in French, which had been brought in to the General. Waterfield further told me that young Mackenzie of our regiment had already volunteered to take a party of the men who had remained loyal, and proceed to their rescue; but that the General had objected to so young an officer going by himself. I at once volunteered to accompany him, and my offer was accepted. I found the party all ready, and mounting a troop-horse, we started, merely putting a few biscuits into our pockets, as we felt we had no time for further preparation. That ride was perhaps the most adventurous one in my career: our intelligence was most vague, and our only reliable information was that the objects of our search were somewhere in the vicinity of Delhi. I shall never forget the heat of that day—it was awful! Parched with thirst, we could only allay our craving for moisture from country wells, the water of which was brackish and bad. Our men behaved right well, for with them it was a great test of endurance and loyalty. At most of the villages the inhabitants turned out against us, and here and there shots were fired at us. But we held to our search, and slowly and by degrees tracking the fugitives, through information scantily and unwillingly given by the villagers, we ran them to ground towards evening, they having taken refuge in a large village called Hurchundpore. As we approached this village, a very large and fortified one, we could see the inhabitants lining the walls. Knowing for a certainty that our fugitives were there, we could not understand these signs of hostility. I rode forward with Mackenzie and a trumpeter, halting our party some way off. Some of the leading inhabitants then came out to parley. Seeing two British officers, they became to a certain extent friendly, but they would not allow us to enter the village with our party, nor would they admit that the fugitives were there. We subsequently ascertained the reason of the villagers' opposition to our approach—which was that, owing to the light blue or French-grey uniform of the men, they believed we were a party of mutineers of the 3rd Light Cavalry, who had been sent from Delhi to intercept the fugitives, and were therefore prepared to give us a hostile reception. After some discussion they said they would allow us, the two British officers, to come into the village, stipulating that our escort should not accompany us. To this we agreed, and after telling the native officers the result of our conference, I desired them to remain outside till we could give them further orders. Mackenzie and I then placed ourselves in the hands of the villagers, who guided us through the narrow lanes of the village. Surrounded by armed men on all sides, whose disposition, judging by their talk and gesticulations, seemed to us far from friendly, the moment was an anxious one. At last, after much delay and passing through narrow lanes, we came to the gates of a *serai*, or walled enclosure, in which the principal house of the village stood. As we entered we realised, to our intense relief and delight, that we had been successful and our search was at an end. For there, grouped in the centre of the enclosure, was a large party of our fellow-countrymen and women, who hailed our advent with an intensity of joy and relief which it is impossible to describe. There were between twenty-five and thirty of them, officers with their wives and daughters, tradesmen, and others. It was a pitiable sight to behold! These poor creatures for a whole week had been wandering about from village to village, spoiled of what few valuables they had, their clothing all torn to shreds, many without shoes, and burnt by the sun to the absolute peeling of their skins, starved and wretched. For a whole week their lives had been scarcely safe for a moment, and now they were saved! Their frantic delight is impossible to describe: they hung about us, embraced us, and called us their saviours. There was no end to their excited feelings. To us, needless to say, it was also a moment of intense happiness to know we had been the means of rescuing them from the almost hopeless condition they were in. News had already been taken into Delhi of their having found refuge in the village, and it was momentarily expected hostile parties would be sent out in search of them. Our next object was to bring in our own men—to which, of course, there was no longer any objection raised — but I grieve to say that during our short absence two had deserted! Our men and horses were then carefully tended and refreshed, and I proceeded to make arrangements for an early return to Meerut.

The headman of the village, curiously enough, turned out to be an old German, named Cohen, who many years before had come to India as an adventurer, and, as was then frequently the case, had settled in the country, married a native woman, and was to all intents living as a native zemindar or cultivator on a large scale. He had a grown-up family, who were brought up as natives; and he himself, from long residence, and dressed in the clothes of his adopted country, could with difficulty be distinguished from a native.

But his treatment of our fugitives and ourselves showed he had not lost the feelings of a Christian and a European. We fared sumptuously that night, and whilst we slept he made arrangements with his sons and the other principal inhabitants for as comfortable a transport for our poor people as could be improvised. By early morning all preparations were made, the majority of the fugitives finding carriage in native *ekkas*, bullock-carts, &c. We then escorted them back safely into Meerut and without any molestation, though for some time we had apprehensions lest a pursuing force from Delhi might catch us up. But we saw nothing, and glad we were when our responsibilities ceased and they were all safely housed in the *Dumdumma* or intrenched position in Meerut. I am glad to say the zemindar Cohen received a very handsome reward from Government in the shape of a large *jagheer* or grant of land, and each man of our rescuing party received promotion or reward of some kind. During the latter years of my service in India I frequently came across two of these men, Jemadar Bisseshur Sing and another, who had received commissions as native officers in Murray's Jat Horse, now the 14th Bengal Lancers, and who often recalled that day's adventure to my memory. One died previous to my leaving India, the other retired on a pension about the time I left the country.

Efforts were now made to organise small expeditions into the neighbouring villages. A body of mounted volunteers was raised from among the civilians and merchants of the station. It was called the "Meerut Light Horse," and they did a certain amount of good service; but the men sadly lacked the knowledge of their weapons, now possessed by the numerous corps of volunteers in India. Were another such emergency to arise there, it is a relief to think that each station would be able to turn out a body of equipped and efficient volunteers, who could undertake all the necessary requirements of "defence." For myself, I was placed in command of a body of irregular horse, composed of men of native cavalry regiments, who had been on furlough at their homes at the time of the outbreak and had come in to Meerut to offer their loyal services: with these men I was able to do some useful work outside the cantonments, patrolling the country in the surrounding districts. It was hard and trying work sometimes, with never a tent to protect us from sun or rain, marching thirty or forty miles a day; but it served to keep me employed. I was always fretting to be away to join the forces now assembling for the attack on Delhi. The army which was detailed for this operation was organised at Umballa, under the immediate command of General Anson, the Commander-in-Chief in India, and was advancing direct on Delhi *viâ* Kurnal; at the same time a force was despatched towards Delhi from Meerut by the Grand Trunk road. This force was under the command of Brigadier Archdale Wilson, C.B., and consisted of the Carabiniers (two squadrons), 60th Rifles, Tombs' Troop of Bengal Horse Artillery, and two heavy guns under Major Alfred Light. They had two most successful engagements with the mutineers, at the Hindun river and Ghazioodeen-Nuggur; and after the latter, under orders from the Commander-in-Chief, marched across by Bhagput to join the main force at Badlee-Ka-Serai, arriving in time to take part in the action at that place, resulting in the defeat of the rebels and the occupation of the now famous ridge in front of the city of Delhi. These were glorious and stirring battles: we could distinctly hear the booming of the guns as our forces were engaged, and every day my blood boiled to be allowed to share in all that was going on.

But my time was to come: I had

suddenly received an order to proceed with a detachment of my men, about twenty-five or thirty sabres, by a forced march to Bijnore, a large native town under civil executive charge, whence the head civilian, Mr Shakespear, had sent in an urgent appeal for help. The distance was forty-five miles, which we did in one march. On arrival I found Mr and Mrs Shakespear, and one other young civilian, Mr G. V. Palmer. They had no troops whatever, only a few native police; but such was the moral effect of their presence that so far all was well, and the Government treasure, amounting to about two and a half lacs of rupees, still safe. This latter Mr Shakespear had caused to be thrown down into a well in the Kutcherry compound. Everything was in a most unsettled and dangerous state. The Nawab of Nujibabad, a neighbouring state, who had so far remained loyal, was known now to be wavering, and Mr Shakespear felt he could no longer rely on his loyalty, hence the appeal to Meerut.

This, then, was our first object, and having quickly annexed some of the Rajah's elephants, we with much difficulty fished up the treasure, in one thousand rupee bags, and having laden our elephants with as much as we could carry, I prepared to return. But before starting I most earnestly begged Mr Shakespear to return to Meerut with me, together with his wife and young Palmer; but nothing would induce this brave man to leave his post, nor would his wife leave him. He assured me he had a good retreat open to him when the time and necessity should come, and I am glad to think that they all eventually escaped to the hill station of Naini Tal, not leaving their duties till the very last moment. Few people nowadays are aware of the marvellous devotion and self-sacrifice shown by the civilian officers in the days of the Mutiny. Many sacrificed themselves rather than for one moment desert their posts. Mr Shakespear was but one instance of the bravery and self-sacrifice that were universal. I said "farewell" with many misgivings, and with a strong wish at my heart that I could remain with them. But my orders were imperative, and, even as it was, I had almost delayed longer than I should have done. News had come that the

Rohilkund mutineers were *en route* to Delhi, and that very probably my return journey would be closed to me; and I felt I must make haste, or all my treasure would be lost. Singular to say, although the men I had with me were all strangers to me, being chiefly men of the 4th and 8th Irregular Cavalry, whose loyalty was more than doubtful, I never for one moment felt a misgiving. I was the sole European, little more than a lad, and with small knowledge of natives or their language; still I felt myself to be the commander, in a position of great trust and responsibility, and I fully trusted my men, and not for a moment was that trust misplaced. We had to cross the river near Bijnore by a very doubtful ford: here and there we had to swim both horses and elephants; and then came the long march of forty-five miles back to Meerut. We were obliged to return by a somewhat circuitous route, for it was rumoured that the mutineers had secured the Grand Trunk road. As it was, we were for a long time in their immediate vicinity—a sore temptation to men like mine. They were in no way bound to me by any personal feelings of loyalty or regard, they barely knew me by name, their *bhaibunds* (or comrades) were mutineers and marching in close proximity to us, and they had the temptation of the loot in their very hands. All they had to do was to kill the English lad, their commander, and make their way unmolested to Delhi to join their friends. But not a man wavered in his loyalty or murmured one word of discontent. Through the long and trying forced march they cared for me more as faithful retainers than soldiers. When I ordered a halt, willing hands were ready to feed and rub down my horse, and make me chupatties and procure me a drink of milk, and in fact everything they could do for me they did willingly; and the result was I brought my detachment and my treasure safely into Meerut, where we received a warm welcome from friends, who thought it more than probable I should never have returned. As it was, whether from over-fatigue, exposure, or it may be anxiety, I was completely bowled over, and had to lie up under a sharp attack of fever. Imagine my feelings of regret when I found, on my recovery, that notwithstanding the wonderful proof of loyalty and trustworthiness these men had evinced whilst with me, the whole detachment had a day or two after their return mutinied and gone over in a body to the enemy, leaving their native officer and one non-commissioned officer to return to Meerut and tell the tale. The poor old Ressaldar came to me with tears coursing down his cheeks, and related with shame and grief how he and one man only were left. Why they had spared me and refrained from looting the treasure which was so completely in their hands is difficult and impossible to say: they did not even wait for their arrears of pay, which I had arranged to give them on the very day they bolted. I had been so proud of their loyalty and allegiance to me that their desertion was quite a blow, and more than ever glad I was when an order came from Delhi, towards the latter end of July 1857, appointing me acting adjutant of "Hodson's Horse," a newly-raised body of irregular horse, organised by a man whose name had been well known in the Punjab and Frontier campaigns as a *sabreur* of distinction, the very mention of whom was a proverb and war-cry in the Punjab as "The Great Hodson."

Little time was wasted in getting ready for my real campaigning. I rejoiced to be given the opportunity of fighting the mutineers, and in a few days started for Delhi *viâ* Baghput, with two doctors, and with a small escort of my old regiment under the command of Lieutenant Fairlie. We had no particular adventures on the road — though, of course, until we reached the vicinity of our own camp area, there was a certain amount of danger and excitement. We were rather pushed for supplies on the way, and I have a vivid recollection of our breakfast after crossing the river at Baghput: our supplies were, indeed, so limited that we could only muster amongst four of us one small tin of sardines. It served to flavour the dry chupatties which we carried in our haversacks,—we ate the sardines, and then scooped up the oil with our chupatties with much gusto. Chupatties are proverbially indigestible, but flavoured with sardine oil and "hungry sauce" we found them an excellent and satisfying repast.

On arrival at the camp at Delhi, I at

once found my way to Hodson's quarters and reported myself to him. I shall not readily forget my first interview with this famous man. I found him sitting, booted and spurred, talking to a native, who was one of his spies from Delhi (for he was the chief of the Intelligence Department as well as commandant of his own body of Irregular Horse). He looked up with a quick, sharp glance, which seemed to go through me—as he told me afterwards he "liked my looks"—and then said, "You are just the man I want, Gough: are you fit for a ride?" I promptly said, "Yes, sir" (though as a matter of fact I was rather beat), and he then said, "Well, come along with me—I am going out for a reconnaissance."

I had some breakfast, and we started

with a small body of his men, and had a really long ride, and a good reconnaissance through the enemy's country. We had no adventures, but I was struck with Hodson's marvellous knowledge of the language and the quick way he seemed to extract all the information he wanted, and his great powers of endurance. We returned to the camp quite late that night, having done over sixty miles, and I was glad to be regaled with a good dinner, the best curry and rice I ever tasted, and a bottle of beer. Although Hodson was able to work everlastingly on very little when necessary, at other times he took very good care of the inner man. He seemed much pleased with me during the day, and I slept that night very tired and very happy.

Here I met my brother Charles (now General Sir Charles Gough, V.C., G.C.B.) He had been in Cashmere when the Mutiny broke out, and had quickly hurried back, to find his regiment, the 8th Light Cavalry, disarmed. He then found his way to Delhi, where he was appointed to do duty with the 1st Punjab Cavalry, and afterwards with the "Guides." It was a great pleasure meeting a brother under such circumstances. Time, we found, had made each other older and more of men than when we had parted four years before. We had many a talk of home and of all the stirring events we had each lately gone through.

It is not my object here to write a history of the siege of Delhi and of the various fights which others have so well described. They were usually infantry engagements, and they were daily and severe — not a day passed without a number of casualties; a heavy artillery fire was always kept up from the ridge which commanded the whole of one side of the city, and was at first occupied by the enemy, but from which we drove them out, planting our own batteries on it, and from thence pouring in shot and shell into their camp. Not having a siege-train, we could do no breaching. There were constant sorties made by the garrison of Delhi, and occasional attacks by ourselves, with a view to strengthening our position and to gaining a better one for the assault, to which we were all eagerly looking forward. The work of the cavalry was outposts, picquets, reconnaissances, escorts, &c. —

hard work and most monotonous, and seldom varied by even a brush with the enemy, who avoided us. Had they, with their great command of cavalry, made really vigorous efforts to disturb our communications, we should have had difficulty in preventing them; but their want of enterprise was our salvation.

We had one cavalry outpost to the rear of our position called the Azadpore Picquet. One morning I took my detachment there in relief of a picquet of Punjab Cavalry. The officer in command had just withdrawn his outposts in anticipation of his relief. As I came up, he said, in a tone of brevity for which he was noted, "'Morning! have some gin?" Thanking him and refusing his kind offer, I asked him, "What's the news? any signs of anything?" His reply was, "No, brought in my men"—when suddenly an alarm was raised that the enemy's cavalry were fording the canal close by a broken bridge. I galloped to the front, and sure enough there were a number of sowars moving across single file. As soon as they saw me they went about, and were off far too quickly for me to catch them up, with the canal between us. But I thought it was as well for my silent friend that I was at the moment more ready than he was. Talking of him and his powers of silence, he was known on one occasion, as we were marching down country, never to have opened his lips or made a remark during a long day's march, till, passing by a village, he saw some chickens—a rare article in our commissariat supplies at the time. He made but the one remark (his sole observation during the day), "Fowls!" and lapsed into his usual silence. He was ever afterwards known by the name of "Fowls."

About the middle of August my commanding officer, Hodson, was sent out on a cavalry reconnaissance in the direction of Rhotuk—a notoriously disaffected town, and where, report said, bodies of the enemy were assembled. The force he had with him consisted of his own regiment—"Hodson's Horse"—and two troops of the "Guides" Cavalry, under my brother, Lieutenant Charles Gough. The "Guides," or "Corps of Guides," was one of the best regiments in the Punjab Frontier Force—a force noted for its loyalty and reliability, and which was therefore able and ready to furnish large and most efficient reinforcements to the British troops before Delhi. The "Corps of Guides" was composed of infantry and cavalry, their strength being equal to a battalion of the former and three squadrons of the latter. Their composition was mixed—Sikhs, Punjabis, Mohammedans, Afridis, and other frontier tribes, and even Hindustanis, the latter of whom remained singularly faithful and loyal, even to fighting against their own countrymen. The men were more or less a picked lot, and their experience in war was great, as from early youth they were constantly engaged in frontier warfare, and it might be said of them, every man was a veteran. We were fortunate in having these two troops of this famous corps to serve as a backbone to our somewhat undisciplined and irregular men in "Hodson's Horse," who, brave and dashing as they were, would be none the worse for the steadier example of the more experienced "Guides." We marched out of the Delhi camp on the early morning of August 15th, without tents or camp equipage—which, indeed, would have been very difficult to carry in such rainy weather, the roads, such as they were, being a mere muddy track and almost impassable for camels; and, moreover, a lot of transport would only have delayed our march.

On the afternoon of the second day we approached the large fortified village of Khurkowda. Hodson was aware of the presence of a number of Irregular Cavalry sowars at Khurkowda, which was their home. These men had gone on furlough previous to the Mutiny, and should, if loyal, have returned to their regiments. It was doubtful, perhaps, if they had actually entered into acts of open hostility towards Government; still, from their not having rejoined their regimental headquarters, their disloyalty was distinctly proved. On nearing Khurkowda we were greeted by a native officer of the 1st Irregular Cavalry, whose name I forget, who came out to Hodson, and, I believe, brought out an offering of fruit, as a *nuzzur* or peace-offering towards the representative of the British Government. Hodson declined his gift and at once had him arrested, and he was placed under a guard.

At this time intelligence was brought to us that a number of dismounted sowars were in the village, and had taken refuge in a large house, which was almost a fortress, so impenetrable of access was it. There were other men about, and it was feared they would raise the town. Hodson determined to arrest these sowars also, and on our arrival at the house they were summoned to surrender. I had with me a small party of the Guides, under Ressaldar Kānon Khan,—a very well-known native officer, a Mohammedan. We found the only means of entrance into the house was by way of a low tunnelled passage, into which a man would have to go on all fours to enter. The enemy were at the other end of this tunnel, about six or seven yards off. We at once parleyed with them, trying to induce them to surrender. Kānon Khan even took out his Koran, which he always carried about with him; and he held it out, and offered to swear to them on the holy book—for they also were Mohammedans—that their lives should be spared if they gave themselves up. I remonstrated with him, saying I could not guarantee their lives; but he quite ridiculed the idea of our keeping faith with such *mufsids* (or rebels), saying that an oath to such scoundrels was not a binding one. However, they would not yield, and abused us in every native term of opprobrium. Seeing the impossibility of gaining an entry to the tunnel, I got a ladder and proceeded to scale the wall, which, as soon as they saw, had the effect of causing them to quit their position on the ground-floor and to rush up on to the roof, where they took refuge in a building consisting of two small rooms leading one into the other, with only one door and a small window, which closed with a wooden shutter. Some of our party entered below and rushed up, and I, having scaled the outer wall, had to run along a rather narrow inner wall to get to the place where the rebels were. A rush was attempted; but one or two men were cut down, and Hodson, who had come up, ordered further attempts by direct attack to cease, and the men to keep out of fire-exposure. In the meantime he sent a party up to make an opening in the roof; and, shoving in bales of burning straw, in a short time smoked the men out. They rushed out sword in hand. There were not more than ten or a dozen of them; but they were fighting for their lives, and their charge was a most gallant one, against great odds. A furious *mêlée* ensued; but it lasted only a few minutes, and the enemy were all overpowered and slain—not a man escaped.

An episode occurred during this little fight which I must relate with a feeling of the deepest gratitude to the gallantry of my brother Charles, who fortunately was so near at hand. When the enemy made their desperate rush I was rather in the forefront of the party awaiting them, and in the *mêlée* which took place I was forced backwards, and, suddenly making a false step from the roof on to a lower roof about a foot down, fell or was forced on my knees. While thus half falling, one man made a cut at me with his heavy sword, which cut right down my riding-boot. Another was aiming a better-directed blow, when my brother, seeing my danger, rushed forward and attacked the two, killing both, and thus undoubtedly saved my life. As it was, the hilt of my sword was forced into my wrist by a sword-cut, inflicting a slight wound.

Having disposed of our enemy in this short but rather smart little skirmish on the top of a house — a kind of fighting I have since carefully avoided — we returned to our bivouac; and nothing further occurred, except the trial by a drum-head court-martial of the native officer and other prisoners. They were sentenced to be shot under Hodson's orders. Neither I nor my brother took part in these proceedings, as I was lying down on a *charpoy* (native bed), feeling rather faint and exhausted, and my brother was sitting by me. There has been considerable condemnation of Hodson for his action towards this native officer; but, as there was no doubt of his disloyalty, rendered more open and declared by the resistance of his men, who were all of his own regiment, Hodson was quite justified in his action, and the native officer and those with him fully deserved their fate.

The next day, August 16th, we moved on in the direction of Rhotuk, where Hodson had heard bodies of the enemy were assembling. Our little skirmish of the day before only made us all the more keen to meet an open enemy in the field. Rapidity of movement was not very practicable, owing to the heavy rain, which necessitated our halting for the night at a village some five miles short of Rhotuk. On the morning of the 17th we moved on. Hodson proceeded in advance to reconnoitre, and found a largish body of armed men drawn up by an old fort, who opened fire on him. He then brought up the remainder of his force and charged into them, and drove them into the town, with a loss of some twelve or thirteen men. After the usual precautions and patrols we bivouacked in an open space near the town. All seemed quiet, and the inhabitants brought us out supplies. The next morning, however, we received intelligence that a considerable force of the enemy's cavalry were approaching to attack us. After a slight skirmish we drove them back; but, being reinforced by about a thousand infantry, they again advanced, and Hodson deemed it advisable to retire and so endeavour to draw them out in the open. This we did, retiring by alternate troops — a movement, in the face of an enemy, requiring great steadiness and nerve, and especially difficult to a young corps like Hodson's Horse, but the tried steadiness of the Guides was our backbone and safeguard. The manœuvre was an entirely successful one, and speedily had the desired effect; for the enemy, deceived into the belief that we were about to bolt, came out with a great show of boldness and much shouting and beating of drums. I was in command of a troop of the "Guides," and had with me my friend Kānon Khan, the native officer who was with me at Khurkowda. As we were retiring I saw him take out his small Koran, already alluded to, and begin to mutter his prayers. In my youthful arrogance and ignorance, I rather chaffed him, asking him if he was afraid. He answered, "No, sahib, but a man should always be prepared," a quiet rebuke which I felt I deserved. When the enemy were well out in the open, Hodson ordered the "About and charge," which was most promptly obeyed, and we went with a will and a dash into the masses of the enemy, who, from their vast superiority of numbers, ought to have annihilated us; but our attack was irresistible, their pluck failed them, and they broke and fled! Still we got well home into them in grand style. This engagement was my first in open contest with an enemy, barring slight skirmishes in the vicinity of Delhi, and my first "charge," and how well

I can recall the moment of intense enthusiasm, and feeling of victory in anticipation, which pervaded my very soul as we dashed into the fight! Somehow, that curious feeling of victory already won seems to be the prevailing sentiment in a good home charge, and doubtless goes far towards ensuring the anticipated result. My mare, a present from a brother-officer, was shot in the chest when clearing a small bank, and came down; but the bullet was spent, and she soon recovered herself and went gallantly on in pursuit. Fifty of the enemy's horsemen and many of the footmen were killed and wounded: we pursued them to the walls of the town and utterly scattered them. It was ludicrous to see the number of accoutrements, clothes, and even shoes which the enemy threw away to lighten themselves in their flight.

On August 19th we returned to camp at Delhi, and Hodson received high commendations for the excellent manner in which he had conducted his reconnaissance. We were all (there were five of us), Lieutenants C. Gough, Macdowell, Ward, Wise, and myself, mentioned in despatches, and we were one and all greatly pleased with the results of our expedition.

After our return to Delhi affairs there went on much as before, except that our activity as besiegers was more strongly developed; and with the arrival of the reinforcements from the Punjab, and the siege-train so long and anxiously expected, signs were evident that the longed-for assault was about to take place. The action of Nujuffghur—when the heroic Nicholson totally defeated the rebel force who had gone out in hopes of intercepting the siege-train, capturing all their guns with a comparatively small loss—was a brilliant episode.

After the arrival of the heavy guns, batteries were formed for the bombardment of the town, regular approaches were made, and there was daily and severe fighting.

On the evening of September 13th orders were issued for the assault to take place the next day. The various columns were formed, and great was our excitement. We had been so long sitting before this doomed city, in the most trying heat and with apparently fruitless labour, that the immediate hopes of an end gave us all a most pleasurable feeling. Knowing, as all did, that a desperate struggle was at hand, few probably felt anything but intense excitement and delight. I happened that evening to have a talk with one of our senior native officers, Ressaldar Mān Sing—a grand old Sikh, who himself had fought against us in the Sutlej and Punjab campaign—and we discussed the question of to-morrow's big fight. As the old man was fond of telling the story even to his dying day, to my own boys amongst others, it runs in his words as follows: "Gough Sahib came to me on the day before the assault and said, 'Mān Sing, there is going to be a great battle to-morrow, and we are going to take Delhi. Hodson says he will ride to Jehannum after the Pandies. I wonder how it will end.' I said to Gough Sahib, 'Well, Sahib, wherever Hodson goes we'll all go,' whereupon Gough Sahib said, 'Well, Mān Sing, salaam; then we'll all go to Jehannum together.'"

I cannot vouch for the strict accuracy of this story, but one and all of us were prepared to follow Hodson to the very death—and I am sure there was not a desponding heart in the whole force.

Ressaldar Mān Sing lived to a good old age, saw much more active service, and when he left the army became head official in charge of the Golden Temple at Amritsur—the sacred place of worship of the Sikhs—and was greatly respected and looked up to. He and I were always great friends, and when he died the poor old man sent me a message to come and see him to say farewell. Most unfortunately I was absent from my head-quarters at the time, and when the message reached me he had passed away.

The story of the assault of Delhi has been so efficiently narrated, and, moreover, my object being only to narrate my own personal share therein, I will merely confine myself to that portion in which I took a humble part. The Cavalry Brigade, or a portion of it, under the leadership of Brigadier Hope Grant, C.B., consisting of 9th Lancers, 1st, 2nd, and 5th Punjab Cavalry (one squadron each, and "Hodson's Horse," six hundred in all, the rest of the cavalry being left to guard the camp), was ordered to take up a position on the slope of the ridge facing Delhi and await events. From there we could see and hear all the stirring fighting going on in the breaches, and subsequently within the walls of Delhi.

After a long suspense, during which we remained dismounted, orders were received for the Brigadier to take his cavalry force immediately in front of the Moree Bastion, to make a vigorous demonstration, and thereby prevent the enemy, who were in strong force in the suburbs of Kissin Gunge, and who had already met and repulsed the attack made on them by the Cashmere Contingent, from returning to Delhi and reinforcing their comrades there. We were right glad of the move, for we were tired enough of remaining inactive whilst all the fighting was going on, but I do not think we quite anticipated the trial we should be put to! We promptly took up our new position, and from that moment were exposed to a most severe fire of round-shot, shrapnel, and grape from the walls, to which we could only reply by an equally determined fire from our guns — of which, I think, we had ten in action. It was a most crucial test of discipline and endurance to stand there for hours, losing good men every minute and being able to make no return. The conduct of the 9th Lancers, who formed our front regiment, and with the Horse Artillery bore the brunt of the pounding, was simply glorious, and gave an example to their native comrades of what British pluck and steadiness could do under the most trying circumstances. The Horse Artillery, too, were splendid: they suffered most severely, and their casualties were so heavy that the officers had at last to serve the guns themselves. This again for me was a "first experience." Being steadily shot at is just at first a most unpleasant one, but as I got a little more accustomed to it, it seemed not much worse than being out in the rain without an umbrella; and after a time I lighted my pipe and took matters very easily. It certainly was a critical time, but the movement had the desired effect, and heavily as our brigade suffered, it was satisfactory to know that we had done our duty and had borne a good, if passive, share in the day's fighting. As evening came on we were retired from our position towards Ludlow Castle, where "Hodson's Horse" bivouacked for the night. We then heard from others more of the events of the day's fighting: how nobly the party under Salkeld and Home, of the Bengal Engineers, had blown up the Cashmere Gate under a fire which nearly destroyed the whole party; how gallantly the breach had been assaulted, and how the various columns had gradually worked their way in. When night fell our position was still one of great anxiety, for we barely held our own, and our losses had been very heavy, considering our small force. In fact, so anxious was our Commander, General Archdale Wilson, that it was said he even thought of withdrawing his troops and awaiting further reinforcements. Fortunately wiser counsels prevailed, and we held on. Amongst the killed that day was Lieutenant Salkeld, R.E., and Lieutenant Gambier, 33rd Native Infantry, both of whom were amongst the fugitives that Mackenzie and I rescued on May 19th, and with whom I had since formed a close

GENERAL SIR A. WILSON.

friendship. But the greatest and most universal loss was that of the noble and determined Nicholson, who, mortally wounded, died a few days afterwards, the idol of all soldiers, and one whose death was a loss to the empire. The next day, and for several more, the fighting in Delhi was continuous and severe. The mutineers, after suffering frightful losses, evacuated the city and dispersed in various columns, and Delhi was ours. I was placed in command of a strong picket guarding one of the gates, where I found myself in possession of the camp of the mutinied 60th Native Infantry; and whilst there I heard the news of the king and his sons having taken refuge in Humayoon's tomb, intelligence of which I sent in to Hodson and on which he promptly acted, going out with but a small force of his own men, capturing the old monarch, and bringing him a prisoner into the city where he had so recently held supreme sway (though it was but a nominal one, as he was old and feeble, and but a puppet in the hands of his sons). These miscreants, the real authors of all the horrible barbarities to which our countrymen and women had been subjected, were also captured by Hodson and brought in as prisoners. The story is well known how Hodson shot these princes with his own hands, and for which he has been so much blamed. I was not with him on this occasion: the only other British eyewitness was his second in command, Lieutenant C. Macdowell, who was afterwards killed at Shumshabad. But I heard the whole story from him (Macdowell) directly afterwards, and from Ressaldar Mān Sing and other native officers; and his and their undivided testimony was, that as Hodson with his small escort of only a hundred sabres was approaching Delhi, the natives crowded round in such numbers, and made such unmistakable signs of attempting a rescue, that the only step left was their death. As Macdowell said, "Our own lives were not worth a moment's purchase." I confess I have never felt anything but regret that Hodson should have taken on himself the part of executioner,—a position unworthy of so brave a man. The wretched princes, cowards and miscreants as they were, deserved their fate, and I have always held that Hodson was right in all he did, only excepting that one false step.

It is said there was an ancient prophecy among the Sikhs that Delhi should fall by their arms, and that her royal princes should be exposed in her public streets; and the men of "Hodson's Horse," when they saw the bodies of these men exposed on the Kotwali of the city, fully believed the prophecy had been fulfilled.

A very curious incident occurred just before I left Delhi. A prisoner was brought into our camp: I believe he was captured when Hodson took the princes — at any rate, he was under a guard of "Hodson's Horse." Strong suspicion pointed to his being a European, though dressed in orthodox native clothes, all white, with the Mohammedan cut of *chupkun.* He was a tall, sturdy-looking man, with a naturally fair face, though extremely sun-burnt, and a fine, soldier-like figure. Repute had been rife in our camp during the siege that more than one European had been on the side of the mutineers; and several officers and men had declared they had noticed a white face among the artillerymen on the Moree Bastion; but few really believed such could be the case. Here, however, was the fact developed, for on close examination the prisoner confessed that he was a European! He gave his name, and stated that he had been sergeant-major of a regiment of native infantry quartered at Bareilly or Moradabad; that when his regiment mutinied they compelled him by force and threats of instant death to accompany them to Delhi; and that when there he was still further compelled to serve their guns against us, for he never could find an opportunity of escaping, being strictly guarded and in daily fear for his life. He added that when Delhi was taken he fled for fear of our vengeance. I know these facts, as I took down the man's depositions: I cannot remember his name, but think it was "Gordon." He gave his evidence, all telling so against himself, in a most independent manner, and without fear. Notwithstanding his own admissions, and the fact of his having fought against us, something in his manner and bearing impressed me in his favour, and I felt pity for him. Criminal as his conduct had been, there was nothing craven about him, and I was glad when I heard his life was to be spared. I do not know what eventually became of him: I left Delhi a day or two after, and the matter dropped out of my memory. Although there have been other reports of our countrymen having joined the rebels, I am strongly of opinion this is the only authenticated case, and I would fain believe that an Englishman does not readily save his life by treachery.

During the few days I remained at Delhi after its fall, I made several expeditions into the city, and there saw the ravages that had been caused by the bombardment, and noticed what a hard struggle it had been for both sides. There was in the palace any amount of beautiful and costly things. A prize committee was quickly formed, and each man got his share according to his rank: my own private loot, if such it could be called, consisted of a sword taken from one of the princes, which Hodson gave me, and which I now possess.

Soon after all these events a wing of "Hodson's Horse" was ordered to accompany Brigadier Greathed's column in pursuit of the Delhi mutineers, who had retreated down the Grand Trunk road, on their way to Oude and Rohilkund. To my great joy Hodson selected me to command the detachment. Thus I was placed in an independent command when under four years' service, and given an opportunity such as seldom falls to an officer so young and, I fear, inexperienced. The cavalry of Greathed's force consisted of the 9th Lancers, 1st, 2nd, and 5th Punjab Cavalry (detachments), each under Lieutenants John Watson, Dighton Probyn, and Younghusband respectively, with the wing of "Hodson's Horse" under myself — my subaltern being Lieutenant G. A. A. Baker of the late 60th Native Infantry. Colonel Ouvry, commanding the 9th Lancers, was in command of this brigade, with Captain H. A. Sarel as brigade major. Our senior officer of the four detachments of Irregular Native Cavalry was John Watson of the 1st Punjab Cavalry, and to him we all looked up as our own immediate Brigadier. A finer officer never breathed—cool, dashing, and intrepid. Probyn was next senior : his name is still a motto in the Bengal Cavalry as one of the most gallant *sabreurs* that service has ever known.

In a few days the column reached Bolundshuhur, where report said the enemy intended to make a stand. This they did, and a very decisive action was there fought, which ended in their complete rout. A considerable force of the mutineers, composed of troops who had retreated from Delhi, were in a strong position near the town of Bolundshuhur, and commanding the approach thereto along the Grand Trunk road. They had also the assistance of a native force under the Nawab of Malaghur, who had for months held sway over that district. Our guns came into action first, pounding the enemy's artillery with such effect that the latter were soon silenced, when our whole force advanced, the infantry speedily forcing the sepoys to abandon their position and retire. The cavalry advancing in co-operation, their retreat soon became a rout, and they were pursued with considerable slaughter. I had an opportunity of testing the qualities of my men in a charge, and was much pleased at their pluck and dash; for, while working along the right flank of our infantry, then in engagement, I came across a superior body of the enemy's cavalry, who at first showed signs of fight, but my men advanced with such spirit that they declined the shock and fled, and we were only able to gather up a few stragglers.

It was at Bolundshuhur that my recollection brings back my first meeting with one who has since made for himself one of the most famous names in modern history, and who has been almost ever since one of my warmest friends. Riding about with orders, and in the very thick of wherever danger was rifest, was a slight, striking-looking, keen young officer, mounted on a Waziri horse, who attracted my notice and made an impression that has kept that meeting fresh in my mind. It was Lieutenant Fred. Roberts, D.A.Q.M.G., then best known as "Bobs," and now Field-Marshal Lord Roberts, V.C., G.C.B.

At the close of the action I was ordered to proceed at once, reconnoitre the fort of Malaghur, in the neighbourhood of Bolundshuhur, and, if evacuated, to seize it. On arrival I found the cage was empty and the birds had flown, but they had left everything behind them. The Nawab of Malaghur had been a noted rebel, who from the very first had risen against the Government, and had, during the five months of anarchy that prevailed, been a general freebooter on the Grand Trunk road, amassing a vast amount of loot, and doing great damage to life and property. In his fort any amount of this latter was found; and his godowns, stored with wines, beer, sugar, and other loot, were a sight to behold. I was young and foolish, I suppose, and did not make use of my opportunity, or I might have commenced feathering my own nest most comfortably. I contented myself with taking a certain amount of necessary stores for our march, and left the loot behind me. I did, however, get one most useful article. On our way to Malaghur Fort I came across a bullock *shigram*, or light, easy, covered spring-cart, drawn by a pair of fast-trotting Dekkan bullocks, which had been deserted by its owner, who had evidently been a gentleman of luxurious tastes, for it was richly lined and with cushions, &c. This I annexed, feeling grieved he had not left his valuables in it. It turned out a most useful find, as it easily carried all my baggage, and the trotting bullocks were able to keep up with the regiment wherever and at whatever pace we marched. In the Nawab's private apartments I found a silver bath, and as there was any amount of rose-water in large glass bottles, I indulged in the luxury of a scented bath therein, which was a treat I have never since had the opportunity of enjoying. Lieutenant Home, R.E., one of the engineer officers who had assisted in blowing up the Cashmere Gate at Delhi, had accompanied me; and next day, pursuant to orders, we spent in blowing up the bastions of the fort and otherwise dismantling it. Alas, poor Home! Such a good fellow and such a gallant officer, his fate was sealed at this miserable little fort. As I was marching out with my detachment in the evening on relief, he was about to blow up one more mine. He begged me to stay and see it, but I could not leave my men. I had scarcely marched off with my detachment, when in the distance I saw and heard the explosion. With it was blown up poor Home himself, the best and cheeriest of good fellows, and one whose gallant deeds would have won him even a greater name than he had already made. I was greatly distressed, for in our short acquaintance at Delhi we had become great friends. And all that day at Malaghur we had been together in what we looked upon as quite a lark, blowing up the old fort, so that I felt almost guilty in not having remained to see the last of the explosions, as he so pressed me; but who can foretell the inevitable, or who could foresee such a result? It seemed an especially hard fate that the gallant Home, who had so justly gained the coveted Victoria Cross in blowing in the Cashmere Gate under such a murderous fire, from which he was one of few survivors, should have met his death in a similar act, but under such very dissimilar circumstances.

It was on my return to camp that I

heard of the death of another very great friend—Lieutenant Lisle Phillips, of the 11th Native Infantry, killed by a bullet in his forehead, almost one of the last shots fired at Delhi. My first acquaintance with Phillips was formed a little before the Mutiny, when I rode a then well-known chestnut Waler horse of his, "Tearaway," in a steeplechase at Lucknow. I had a very severe fall, which nearly ended my existence. His regiment came to Meerut, and after the Mutiny Phillips was attached to the 60th Rifles and went with that battalion to Delhi, where his gallantry and *bonhomie* made him so popular in the regiment that the colonel recommended him for a permanent commission in the 60th. When his death occurred the orders were actually out posting him to the first battalion 60th Rifles. Poor fellow, he had a presentiment he would not survive the siege, for on saying good-bye to me at Meerut, he told me he had made his will, leaving me his steeplechaser "Tearaway," who had given me so bad a fall, but which had been the foundation of our friendship. I received intimation of the will from Dr Innes, the well-known medico of the 60th, and a day or two afterwards "Tearaway" overtook me, and right well he carried me through many a long day's work and many a rough-and-tumble fight, till at last, good old horse, he was shot under me at Lucknow.

III.

AFTER the action of Bolundshuhur, Greathed's column (as our force was called) continued its march down country. In all directions there were manifest tokens of the anarchy that had prevailed during the previous four or five months. Everything belonging to or bearing any trace of British rule had been ruthlessly destroyed. At Bolundshuhur the Government buildings and bungalows had been burned, there was no traffic on the public roads, the telegraph posts and wire had been taken away, and even the milestones had been broken and thrown down. Our wooden telegraph-posts were fixed in iron sockets about three feet long, to protect the wood from the ravages of white ants. The ingenuity of the rebels had converted these iron sockets into miniature cannon, cutting up the telegraph wire as ammunition. In some of our smaller fights these queer little guns were used against us, but I cannot say that I ever heard of any serious casualty being caused by the "telegraph guns," as they were called.

Our route lay down the Grand Trunk road; all our hopes and aspirations breathing the one watchword "Relief of Lucknow," where Havelock's gallant little force, having succeeded in the face of enormous difficulties in effecting a junction with the beleaguered garrison there, and relieving them from their immediate and almost certain danger of annihilation, were themselves besieged. It was necessary for us to overcome all opposition by the way, and our first obstacle was encountered at the village of Akrabad, near Allyghur, where a large body of rebels was assembled under the leadership of two noted and influential Rajpoot zemindars. The four detachments of Native Cavalry were sent on ahead rapidly, with orders to surround the village and cut off all escape, which was most effectively accomplished. The infantry coming up took the place by assault, but there was no determined opposition, and the rebels broke and fled, only to fall into the hands of the surrounding cavalry. There was not much excitement over the affair,—and I only mention it here as we succeeded in killing the two leaders (brothers), very fine stalwart men, whose bodies were brought into the village and exposed in the market-place for identification. By a curious coincidence, which I only discovered many years after, the third brother (then a native officer in the 17th Irregular Cavalry—which regiment mutinied, while he, fortunately for himself, remained faithful) came in for all the property, which was assigned to him by Government as a reward for his loyalty. This man years afterwards was the Ressaldar major of my regiment, the 12th Bengal Cavalry, and one of the finest native officers of the old stamp I have ever come across. His name was Jowahir Sing: he eventually retired from the service with a large pension, and the title of

Sirdar Bahadur, to live in his *jagheer*, this same village of Akrabad. He and I often compared notes of the events of the Mutiny days; and I don't think he ever bore me the slightest grudge for having taken part in the action which resulted in the death of his two brothers and his own good fortune! I went once to buy remounts in his district (a great horse-breeding one), and stayed the night at his village, and he took quite a keen interest in my account of the cavalry action I have here mentioned.

Whilst our force was encamped at Allyghur, where also we had some desultory fighting, urgent news came from Agra calling for immediate reinforcements, as a large body of mutineers was threatening that important city from the direction of Gwalior and Dholepur. In fact, the call for relief was so urgent that our whole force made a forced march on to Agra (doing the last fifty miles in twenty-eight hours), hoping and expecting to have a good fight the next day. We arrived on the morning of October 10th. As our advanced cavalry passed over the bridge of boats, immediately under the imposing fort of Agra, all seemed curiously quiet and peaceful, nothing in the least indicating that an enemy could be anywhere in the vicinity—and such, to our disappointment, we were informed by the local authorities was the case. The mutineers, it was asserted, having learnt of our approach, had retired, and not a sign of them was to be seen or heard of.

But a great surprise was in store for us: as soon as our camp site was pointed out to us, and I had seen the men dismounted and picketing their horses, I rode up to the fort, having accepted with many others an invitation to breakfast with an old chum in the commissariat—a known provider of all that was good; and I was just sitting down to a quiet, square meal when the sound of guns boomed suddenly and rapidly in our ears. There was no mistaking the sound: they were guns in action, as at such a time no powder was wasted on salutes. To jump from the table and mount our horses was the work of an instant, and we galloped down to the camp. There was great commotion and much firing going on. The enemy, who had never left their ground, were upon us, and their cavalry had made a rush through to our camp. We got to arms in an incredibly short space of time and attacked them. In their turn they seemed to be quite surprised at our presence, thinking they had only the Agra force to oppose them: though they fought very pluckily at first, they were as usual beaten, and having made no arrangement for a retreat, lost every one of their guns and left a number of killed and wounded. But the *mêlée* soon was over, and the rest of the action was a pursuit, varied by many single fights; for though "John Pandy," as we styled the mutinous sepoy, would not stand up against us as a body, their individual gallantry was undeniable, and many men fought like heroes when driven to bay. The pursuit only ceased at the banks of the river — the Kala Nuddee, I think it was called. By that time we were all pretty tired, but seeing on the opposite side some of the enemy's cavalry, who in full confidence of their safety with the river between us had begun to wave their swords in defiance (my wrath, moreover, being additionally fired by seeing that they wore the hated French-grey uniform so lately my own), I proceeded with my men to cross the river by a ford, and once over we soon put an end to their swagger. Amongst their losses was a leader of rank who was trying to escape in an *ekka* (light country cart). My men brought me back his gold collar, a badge of rank worn by all native officers of the old Company's army, proving him to have been a soubadar major of an infantry regiment. This badge was afterwards stolen with other things from my tent. I made a sad mistake that day: when fording the river I again came across a fine bullock *shigram* which had been abandoned by its owners in their hasty flight, but which I passed by, partly in my anxiety to get to the opposite bank, and possibly because I had previously annexed a similar cart at Bolundshuhur. I heard afterwards that this cart and its contents, which were very valuable, fell into another's hands, and I had but the regret of having missed a golden opportunity!

This action of Agra was a marvellously successful one in all its results. Surprised, in the first instance (for we were undoubtedly caught napping, in fancied security in the absence of our enemy), regiments having no preconcerted plan of action had to fight their own battle according to their position as they stood in the encamping-ground, and dispose of their immediate enemy as best they could. Most fortunately they were thoroughly accustomed to sudden attacks, and all behaved right well. Equally fortunately, the enemy did not appear to be under any organised system of attack, and the result of the *mêlée* was quickly fatal to them. The 9th Lancers, the first regiment on whom the attack took place, behaved splendidly, as they always did; but one squadron, which bore the first brunt, suffered very severely, losing two officers—Captain French killed, and Lieutenant Jones desperately wounded and almost cut to pieces. His recovery was a marvel to all, and his subsequent decoration of the Victoria Cross was well earned and deserved. I was well pleased with the behaviour of my men on this occasion. They had very readily pulled themselves together when the first alarm took place, and behaved with considerable dash. It was always necessary to bear in mind that these men were utterly undisciplined and untaught soldiers according to our ideas, being either raw recruits, or disbanded soldiers of the old Khalsa army, who had fought against us in the Punjab some eight years previously. They were indifferent riders, as Sikhs usually are (till taught), and at least half of them used with one hand to clutch hold of the high knob in front of the Sikh saddle as they galloped along. They had no knowledge of drill or of our words of command; in fact, all I attempted to teach them were, "Threes right" or "Threes left" (never Threes about!), and "Form Line," "Charge." However, with all their want of knowledge and training, they had plenty of pluck, and their success lay in that, combined with readiness and goodwill for any amount of work. In strong contrast to my men was the discipline and turn-out of the three detachments of Punjab Cavalry, under Watson, Probyn, and Younghusband. These regiments were the nucleus of the famous Bengal Cavalry of the present day—the finest and most efficient Light Cavalry in the world. It was on this occasion that Lieutenant Younghusband had a singularly narrow escape. During a charge he and his horse suddenly disappeared down a blind well. He was quickly followed by a mounted sowar, and by yet another. The well probably was almost dry, but the fall itself and the shock of the others falling on him must have been awful; yet, strange to say, Younghusband was taken out alive, the sole survivor of the men and horses that went down. He was taken to hospital terribly bruised, but made a rapid recovery, and was able to accompany the force down country. Brigadier Hope Grant of the 9th Lancers joined the force after leaving Agra, and took the command from Brigadier Greathed as senior officer. I believe it was never quite settled which of the two brigadiers, Greathed or Cotton (the latter commanding the Agra Brigade), could claim the honour of the victory on October 10th, for they both sent in despatches. But as all the work was done by our force, and we were then under Greathed's orders, we, who were chiefly concerned, always gave him the credit of being the leader. Had it been a reverse instead of a victory, I doubt if there would have been very keen claims for the responsibility. After the battle of Agra the force proceeded down country in pursuit of its original plan for the relief of Lucknow. I was told off to escort a large convoy of camels with supplies, which were being collected by the indefatigable commissariat officer at Agra, my old friend Chalmers, the same with whom I was breakfasting in the fort when the alarm first sounded on the 10th. These were quickly collected, to my great satisfaction, and I hastened after the force. I had left at Allyghur one hundred sabres under Lieutenant G. A. A. Baker, thereby reducing my detachment to about two hundred and fifty. At Agra a new subaltern was attached to me — Lieutenant Craigie-Halkett, from one of the mutinied regiments there — as nice a lad as I ever met, quite a child in looks, but full of go and ardour. Hampered as we were with this large convoy of camels, which extended miles in length, and with only my small force to guard them, I was glad enough to pick up the force again and hand over my troublesome charge. We had occasional skirmishes, but no particular excitement in our march down country, excepting a small opposition near the very ancient and ruined town of Kanouj, in which, however, I had no part.

Just one march before we reached Cawnpore a very unpleasant incident occurred, which caused me great grief at the time, and which I feared would utterly ruin all my chances of distinction, but which, as so many things unexpectedly do in one's daily life, afterwards proved just the reverse. I have already alluded to the undisciplined state of my men, and that their idea of "orders" was about as vague as could be well conceived. Our commander—Brigadier Hope Grant, C.B., a man who had been brought up in the strict routine of the 9th Lancers—could not appreciate the fact that such a "rabble," as he was pleased to term us "Hodson's Horse," could be worth anything as soldiers. As ill luck would have it, on visiting the picquets one afternoon the General (Hope Grant) found the one supplied by "Hodson's Horse" sadly wanting in that alert smartness so dear to the heart of the energetic cavalry commander. He was very angry, and "pitched into" the native officer roundly and justly, as he deserved; and then sent for me, when he gave me as rough a rubbing-up as his naturally kind old heart and tongue was capable of, and, visiting all the sins of my men, who never dreamt they were to blame, on my devoted head, passed the order that the detachment of "Hodson's Horse" under Lieutenant Hugh Gough was to be placed on perpetual rearguard till further orders.

This was a blow and a punishment with a vengeance. There is no duty so irksome, so onerous, or so wanting in opportunity as that of "rearguard." I, in my turn, was naturally very disgusted with my men, and gave them, and especially the native officers, my views on the matter most strongly. They were full of penitence, and vowed they would show what they could do to make up for it on the earliest opportunity. But this was small consolation to me, especially as we were not likely to get the desired opportunity in our unenviable position on the rearguard.

Towards the end of October the column reached Cawnpore, where we found everything very quiet; and, if it had not been for the destruction and desolation around, one would never have believed from the general demeanour of the people that they had ever been in opposition to our rule, whereas the whole city and the general population had sided with the Nana, and had shared in his infamous atrocities. Having myself been staying at Cawnpore only two months before the outbreak of the Mutiny, the sight of the ruined station, the burnt bungalows, and the memory of my old friends murdered under such terrible circumstances, recalled to my mind all the sad events of the past few months. And when I beheld the well and its surroundings, where our poor women and children had been hacked to pieces and their bodies thrown down, my blood boiled for vengeance. Doubtless in these far distant days, when the memory of the deeds of blood and cruelty practised on our people by the treacherous Nana and our own sepoys has faded away, such a sentiment may be condemned; but for any one who had absolutely seen the sword-cuts on the tree over the well, with the stains of blood, and here and there tresses of hair cut into the bark, and who, moreover, had gone through the experiences I had in that first awful night at Meerut, there could be but one thought—vengeance, deep and sure.

One could scarcely believe that so

lengthened a stand could have been made by the small garrison under General Wheeler against such frightful odds, in a miserable intrenchment such as that in which they held their own for so long, and from which they were only dislodged by treachery — inducing a capitulation, whereby our people were placed in the hands of the Nana and his supporters, in whose word and honour they placed their trust. I can only conceive that it was the presence of the women and children and the hope of saving them that induced Sir Hugh Wheeler to capitulate. Alone with his small garrison, he would doubtless have made a strong effort to cut his way through their enemies; and, though they probably would have been destroyed, they would at any rate have sold their lives dearly.

But it was decided otherwise. Trust was placed in the Nana's word, and the result was that the brave little garrison, unarmed and defenceless, was destroyed almost to a man, and the women and children fell into the Nana's hands to meet a later and more cruel death.

Our column, having halted a day or two, awaiting orders from our new Commander-in-Chief—Sir Colin Campbell, who was hastening up country—again moved on our way to Lucknow. We left Cawnpore on October 30th, "Hodson's Horse" still occupying our place of punishment—"perpetual rearguard." For the first two days there was neither fighting nor excitement of any kind. On the third day, however, opposition met the column at the Bunnee Bridge, the passage of which was disputed by the enemy, who were posted in a strong village commanding the bridge. Of course I saw nothing of this fight, being employed in looking after the safety of the baggage and hustling up the camels and bullock-carts, which formed a long and straggling line —a task very trying to one's temper and patience, and the more so as one felt so utterly disgusted at being kept out of the good thing going on in front. In fact, I was not amiable. But fortune smiled on me when least expected, and sent an enterprising enemy round by the rear to see what they could do in the way of loot and damage. This party, numbering over two hundred horsemen, suddenly appeared on our left flank, and made a dash towards the line of baggage. Captain Wheatcroft, of the Carabiniers—a gallant officer, who had just come out from England in hopes of joining his regiment at Meerut or Delhi, and who, on reporting his arrival at Cawnpore, had been posted to the Military Train—was then commanding the rearguard. He desired me to reconnoitre the enemy's cavalry, and see what they were up to. I went forward, therefore, with some fifteen troopers, and soon came in full view of the enemy—a body of our own mutinied Irregular Horse—who, seeing the smallness of my party, promptly came at us, and saluted us with a volley from their carbines, which, as they fired from on horseback, was ill directed and harmless. In the meantime I ordered up as many of my regiment as I could quickly gather together, and as soon as I got about forty men, charged them with a tremendous cheer, and soon got into the thick of them. They could not stand the shock of the charge, which we were able to deliver home, and broke and fled. We pursued them some way, and cut up numbers of them. My men were mad to retrieve their disgrace and the rearguard punishment, and behaved most splendidly. Wheatcroft, in the meantime, seeing me disappear over the undulating ground with a cheer and a charge, and knowing our small numbers, was in a desperate state of anxiety and alarm, and was about to start to my assistance, when he saw us returning in triumph and safety. To me this little affair gave the deepest joy, for I felt my men had shown what they could do, and that if they had been slack on picquet duty, they were not slack in a charge. Wheatcroft was full of praise and congratulation, and gave a very flattering report of my little achievement to General Hope Grant, who made amends for all we had suffered by saying he had been mistaken in his estimation of my men, and adding that we should have the post of advance-guard on the march of the force to the Alum Bagh. I slept that night the sleep of the justly happy, and dreamed of Victoria Crosses, brevets, and other chances, which I had thought were closed to me for ever.

We halted a day or two at the Bunnee Bridge, awaiting the arrival of Sir Colin Campbell to take command of the force, now augmented by troops from England —who, though not many, were worth their weight in gold. The first day of the halt the cavalry in camp were employed in scouring the country, scouting everywhere for any bodies of the enemy's cavalry who might be prowling about, and here and there punishing refractory villages, the inhabitants of which had been hostile to us, but who in most cases had wisely quitted their tenements and escaped the results of our search. With a detachment of my regiment I had come to a village known to have been actively hostile, and my orders were to burn it. I found the village apparently empty, and had sent parties to set the houses on fire, waiting myself outside, attended by one orderly, when suddenly a *fakeer* rushed out from a building and came straight at me. His naked body smeared with dust and ashes, and with his long matted hair, he looked a veritable fiend as, armed with a *lathie* or iron-bound stick, he bounded at me with a yell of fury, taking me completely by surprise. I had barely time to take out my revolver—which unfortunately was only a toy weapon presented to me by a lady on my leaving Meerut, and the only pistol I possessed. I promptly fired at him, hitting him full on his left breast, but the wretched little popgun failed to do more than just stagger him, when he again made a bound forward, shouting "*Ham bhi marega, soor!*" ("I also can strike, pig!"), and I had just time to draw my sword and ward off a terrific blow, which almost broke down my guard, but which I returned with such effect that he turned back and fled into the burning village, cursing me loudly as he went. I saw no more of him, and I presume he perished among his gods, without the satisfaction of having gained his passport to heaven through the sacrifice of an infidel. He was a gallant scoundrel; but I cannot say his language was that of a holy man, which according to his lights he aspired to be. The harmless result of my pistol-shot, which, though hitting him directly over the heart, had but staggered him, warned me for the future not to trust in such a miniature weapon, and I took the earliest opportunity to provide myself with a good serviceable Colt's revolver.

The Commander-in-Chief, Sir Colin Campbell, joined us on November 10th, and on the following day he reviewed the force. It was not a very imposing array, as far as numbers went; but it was a veteran little army, fit and ready to go anywhere or dare anything, especially in the cause for which we were fighting. The old Chief made a short speech to each regiment as he passed. When he came to the Punjab Irregular Cavalry, the four detachments of which, under Watson, Probyn, Younghusband, and myself, were drawn up together, he stopped and gave us no end of *kudos*, saying he had heard what good service we had done at Delhi and in the march down country, and complimented the native officers and men. I was more than ever pleased that my own men in particular had distinguished themselves so lately, and had redeemed their character in Sir Hope Grant's opinion.

On November 12th, 1857, the forces under the Commander-in-Chief in India marched on to the Alum Bagh. I now, with my detachment, had the post of honour on the advance-guard, as Sir Hope Grant had promised me should be the case. It was not expected we should meet with opposition, as Havelock's troops held the Alum Bagh; and though they had had constant and severe fighting ever since the first relief of Lucknow, it all came from the direction of the city and the beleaguering enemy. But suddenly, as our column was advancing up the road, an attack developed itself on the right flank, where a body of the enemy, calculated at about two thousand strong, with two guns, had taken up a position, having apparently come out of the fort of Jellalabad. As these guns were troublesome, and perhaps from the wish to give me a chance, the General—for it was Hope Grant who was commanding the advance—rode up to me, and desired me to take my squadron and see if I could capture the guns.

He further gave me an order to spike them if I found I could not get them away; and to carry out this order I was provided with a hammer and spikes, or large nails. Of how I disposed of them I have not the slightest recollection, but I rather suspect I threw them away!

With my small body of men, my only chance of success was by making a flank attack, and if possible a surprise. With this object I made a considerable *détour*, and managed, under cover of some fields of growing corn or sugar-cane, to arrive on the left flank of the enemy perfectly unseen. The guns were posted on a small mound, and a considerable body of the enemy had an admirable position in rear of this mound, in front of and amidst some trees and scrub. Between us and them lay a marshy *jheel*, with long, reedy grass — an unpleasant obstacle, but which served admirably to cover our movements. I then advanced my men through this *jheel* and long grass at a trot, and so concealed our movements till we got clear, when I gave the word "Form line" and "Charge." My men gave a ringing cheer, and we were into the masses. The surprise was complete, and owing to its suddenness they had no conception of our numbers, and so the shock to them and victory to us was as if it had been a whole brigade. My charger "Tearaway," the horse left me in poor Phillips' will, carried me like a bird, and I found myself well ahead. It seemed like cutting one's way through a field of corn, and I had to make a lane for myself as I rode along. The men followed me splendidly, and in a very short time the affair was over,—the guns were captured, the enemy scattered, and the fight became a pursuit. Our loss was very trifling, as is often the case in a sudden surprise, but we cut up numbers of the enemy, and should have accounted for more but for the nature of the ground. I came out of the fight untouched, and this I attribute to the pace I went; but my good horse "Tearaway" suffered, having a sabre-slash over his quarter and another sabre-wound on his foreleg, while my coat-skirt was cut clean through, and the puggeree which, wound round a forage-cap, had been my sole head-dress during the past months, was cut almost to the last fold, but by its thickness undoubtedly saved my head. Two or three staff officers had ridden round, seeing what was going on, and shared in the fight, among them Roberts and Augustus Anson, and, I believe, Captain Mayne (subsequently killed at the attack on the Dilkoosha). Sir Colin Campbell had just ridden up to the front as the affair took place, and witnessed the charge. I was very proud, both for my men and myself, when a little later he sent for me, and, complimenting me highly, said he should be glad to promote any man I would recommend for conspicuous gallantry. Sir Colin Campbell afterwards made particular mention of my name in his despatches, thereby gaining for me the honoured and most-coveted distinction of the Victoria Cross.

The force advanced from the Alum Bagh to the capture of the Dilkoosha (formerly the summer palace of the kings of Oude), and from thence to the Martinière, now known as the Martinière College.[1] There was a great deal of fighting during those two days, and many casualties: amongst them, to my great regret, was the death of Captain Wheatcroft of the Carabiniers. My own share in the fighting was very small, as we were on rearguard both days, but not now as a punishment, only as being on the roster for the day; and its monotony was not relieved by even a desultory charge. The Punjab Cavalry came in for work, as usual, both Watson and Probyn charging gallantly and doing good service. On the evening of the

[1] This fine building was originally built by a French General Martin for a college, for which purpose it is still maintained by the British Government. There are similar institutions in Calcutta, and at Lyons, France.

15th (November) the orders were out for the advance on Lucknow the following day. Having had two days' hard work, and with the prospect of still harder on the morrow, we were just settling down in our camp under some trees in the Martinière inclosure, having fed and watered our horses, when I received an order to accompany with my men a staff officer who was returning to the Alum Bagh, to bring up the reserve rifle ammunition, which had most unaccountably been left behind when the force advanced the previous day. Lieutenant Younghusband, commanding the squadron 5th Punjab Cavalry, also formed part of the escort. The staff officer who carried the orders was Lieutenant Frederick Roberts. Starting by night, we took the route by which our force had advanced. After passing the Dilkoosha, some doubt arose as to our proper road: there was very little in the shape of "road" at all to guide us. Roberts, however, produced a compass, and with its aid we arrived safely at the Alum Bagh, took over charge of the ammunition, and returned to our camp in time to take part in next day's proceedings. Younghusband held to his opinion that the road lay in the contrary direction. He eventually arrived there, but not till after we had left on our return march. On the morning of November 16th, 1857, the force under Sir Colin Campbell advanced to the relief of Lucknow, leaving a strong garrison at the Dilkoosha and La Martinière. On this occasion my detachment was the advance-guard. After marching about a mile we came to a thick jungle, with only a narrow lane through trees and shrubs. The Commander-in-Chief, who was commanding in person, now ordered up a company of the 53rd Regiment to skirmish through the thicket. After advancing a quarter of a mile farther we came to a village where our skirmishers were fired upon; more infantry were ordered up, and in about another minute the action had begun in real earnest. We found the enemy, who were in great force, had taken up their position in the garden of Secundra Bagh, a pleasure-garden, but walled all round and loopholed for musketry defence. It was evident that this place must be taken before any further advance could be made. And it was still more evident to me that we, "Hodson's Horse," were in a most inconvenient spot: we could neither advance nor retire, for, in the first place, any further progress was rendered impossible by abattis and barricades in front; and in the second, the narrow lane was speedily blocked by infantry and artillery hurrying up to the scene of action. It was indeed a scene of turmoil! Up, too, came the Commander-in-Chief himself. Seeing me and my troopers blocking up the road, and as I said irretrievably "stuck," he wanted to know what we were doing there, and why we did not make way for the infantry and artillery — forgetting for the moment, perhaps, that duty had led us to the front, and abattis and barricades made our moving aside easier said than done: exit there was none, and we had to dispose of ourselves as best we could, but I have seldom found myself so very much *de trop* as I was on this occasion.

In the meantime the infantry had hurried up, and were preparing to assault; but it was necessary to breach the walls first, and for this purpose a troop of Bengal Horse Artillery (Blunt's, I think) was brought up, and soon commenced a furious cannonade on the garden wall at a very short range, point-blank. A couple of Peel's 24-pounder guns were also brought into action, manned by British tars — splendid fellows, to whom fighting seemed but a pastime, and who had excited the intense admiration of our Sikhs when the British reinforcements first joined us. It took a very short time to batter in a considerable breach; and then ensued one of the most exciting scenes I ever witnessed — the 93rd Highlanders and 4th Punjab Infantry racing like mad to be first in the breach.

At this time I and my men were under cover of a mud wall, which in a measure protected us from the fire of the rebel force which lay between us and Lucknow, but in full view of all that occurred in the taking of the Secundra Bagh. It was a most stirring sight, and I confess at this moment I longed to be in with them and free from my forced inaction. I could not well say which won the race for the breach, Sikh or Highlander — at any rate, they went in shoulder to shoulder. The story is well known how they forced their way in, and the opposition they met with; for at the first rush the invaders could only enter in limited numbers, but those who did, made their point good, and the stream of attack strengthening every moment, ground was gained at every step; and almost in less time than it has taken me to describe the scene, the Secundra Bagh was captured. But the fighting continued for some time. The enemy had no retreat, they knew they would receive no quarter, and so they fought in wild despair. Not a man escaped: over seventeeen hundred dead bodies lay in that small walled inclosure, and I believe every man among them a mutineer How long the conflict actually lasted I cannot say, but I can never forget the continual roll and rattle of musketry, the cheers and shouts of the victors, and the cries of the vanquished: as it gradually ceased, and a comparative silence ensued, varied by occasional shots or a section volley, or sudden roll of independent firing, one realised that a great triumph had been won that day by British pluck and British steel.

After the capture of Secundra Bagh I was ordered to join the remainder of the cavalry force, occupied in watching and guarding our flanks and communication — a work certainly more suited to our capacities than being involved in the midst of an infantry action — where, though never actively engaged, we were exposed to a considerable fire during the day, and I had to deplore the loss of my subaltern, young Craigie-Halkett, who, struck by a fragment of shell in the spine, was mortally wounded, and died after a month of great suffering. A right gallant lad, he had joined me at Agra but a short time before, and now his career was closed. Our other casualties were three or four sowars wounded and one killed.

The troops were now rapidly pushed up to advance on Lucknow. Despatches and history have related, better than I could possibly describe, all the events that led up to the final relief of Lucknow, telling not only the deeds of that brave little garrison, which with its gallant commanders, Sir Henry Lawrence and Brigadier Inglis, had endured so much, but also of that heroic force which, under Outram and Havelock, had successfully fought their way to Lucknow in the face of frightful odds and under such trying conditions.

But the relief was accomplished; next day our commanders joined hands; and great must have been our old Chief's satisfaction at the result of his hard fighting, and greater still the delight of the brave generals, whose anxieties had been so overwhelming. Sir Henry Lawrence, alas! had been killed in the early part of the siege.

It was a great and real grief to the whole army when, a day or two afterwards, we heard that the noble Havelock had succumbed to the illness which had seized him immediately after the Relief, and almost before he had time to realise that he had gained the reward of all his toil, anxiety, and valour. But his great name has lived, and will live for ever, in the heart of every soldier.

Sir Colin Campbell now decided on the evacuation of Lucknow, finding he had not a sufficiently large force to hold it and at the same time carry out his plan of relieving the North-West Provinces, where the mutinous pest was still in the ascendant. The next few days were therefore spent in removing the sick and wounded, the ladies and children, and such military stores as were worth the removal, to the Dilkoosha. I took the opportunity to visit the long-beleaguered Residency two or three times; my only previous visit to Lucknow having been about two months before the outbreak of the Mutiny, when I had gone there for a festive gathering, races, balls, and such-like, and when I had made many friends and met with much kindness. On my present visit how changed was everything! Those who had entertained me so kindly a short time before were now destitute, houses and homes burnt and pillaged, and they themselves had been for months enduring hardships and privations which few in our happy England can realise: women and children exposed to all the trials of an Indian climate, aggravated by hunger and sickness, and want of even the ordinary necessities of life, with continuous fighting and slaughter around them, and all the horrors of a siege. Of those I had known, some had lived through these miseries, but many had succumbed. Glad were those who were left to see us and hear news of the outer world, and thankful to receive the few creature comforts we could bestow. We had but little, but, needless to say, that little was freely given.

On November 22nd we evacuated the Residency, with all the buildings we had taken, and the combined forces were concentrated at the Martinière and the Dilkoosha. On the 25th we commenced our retirement towards Cawnpore, leaving a strong force at Alum Bagh, under the command of Sir James Outram.

Scarcely had Sir Colin's force marched from the Alum Bagh when news reached us of severe fighting at Cawnpore, and the necessity of a forced march for the relief of the force there, which, under the command of General Wyndham, of Redan fame, had met with a serious reverse in an engagement with a vastly superior force of the enemy, composed chiefly of the Gwalior Contingent, a small army kept up by the Maharajah of Gwalior under treaty with the British Government, on much the same lines as the present Hyderabad Contingent, being drilled and officered by British officers, but paid by the Maharajah. This contingent had mutinied some months previously, killing some of their officers, the remainder of whom escaped to Agra. They had remained intact as a separate force, and had now advanced against Cawnpore from Calpee; and knowing the weakness of our garrison there, their object was to take Sir Colin in rear, and overcoming the weaker force under Wyndham, to cut us off in our retirement from Oude. They had so far succeeded that, having beaten Wyndham in the open, they had driven him into his intrenchments, and had taken possession of the city of Cawnpore, and so for a time were masters of the situation. But not for long! As soon as Sir Colin heard of Wyndham's reverse he made all haste to his relief, though, being impeded by the large convoy of sick, wounded, and the impedimenta brought out of the Residency, our progress was not so quick as we would have wished.

The duties of the cavalry on this return march were very heavy, our numbers were few, and we had a large convoy to guard. But our progress was unimpeded, and we duly reached Cawnpore; and as we recrossed the bridge of boats, being pounded at by a battery of the enemy's guns, we felt we were in for another good thing, and blessed our lucky stars accordingly. We found General Wyndham's small garrison safely maintaining their intrenched position, but absolutely shut up therein, having lost their camp and camp equipage.

The arrival of Sir Colin's force quite

altered the state of affairs: the enemy took up a more respectful position as regards distance and attitude, and from being the aggressive party had to assume the defensive.

As soon as carriage could be procured, the Chief wisely determined to despatch everything in the shape of impedimenta to Allahabad; and thankful must have been the feelings of the poor ladies and the sick and wounded when their faces were turned towards home—though the convoy of so valuable a freight must have been a source of much anxiety to those who were placed in charge.

During the few days' delay at Cawnpore we had a certain amount of skirmishing and occasional cannonading, which served to keep up our spirits, knowing that a better time was coming.

My detachment of "Hodson's Horse" was encamped not far from the "Savāda Kotee," the large house which had been occupied by the Nana when he was besieging the ill-fated Wheeler in his so-called intrenchment, and where, I believe, at one time our women and children had been imprisoned, after the wholesale massacre of Wheeler's garrison.

The enemy's cavalry day picquets were posted not far from us, and we used constantly to go out and try to tempt them into coming into the open,—but they were too shy for a closer acquaintance.

The whole force was right glad when, having started off the convoy in safety to Allahabad, our forced inaction was at an end, and the morning of December 6th again found us in order of battle.

Sir Colin Campbell's dispositions were

very complete. He had a fine force at his disposal, and the enemy was polite enough to wait his leisure. With his infantry and artillery he drove them in great style from all their various positions in and about the Cawnpore cantonments, the cavalry advancing in unison by the flanks, ready to act as occasion afforded. To our disgust, the enemy's cavalry, the well-known Gwalior troops, from whom we had hoped for better deeds, never showed in the action at all, and we had, therefore, to wait the result of the infantry action — about which, however, there was never a doubt, as our brave troops drove the enemy from position after position.

Our time came at last: as the enemy, so proudly victorious over Wyndham but a few days before, now retreated or rather fled towards Calpee, by their former line of advance, we were in and amongst them, driving them before us, a disorganised, flying rabble, and capturing gun after gun as they were left abandoned on the field or on the road: we kept up our pace for full fourteen miles on the Calpee road, seldom drawing rein, and ended by capturing seventeen guns.

Old Sir Colin accompanied the pursuit, and rode alongside me for some time, seeming to thoroughly enjoy the fun, saying, "By Jove! you fellows can go," and adding it was "the very best run" he had ever had. His whole face beamed with delight, and I felt I could have gone anywhere for the plucky old man.

It was very late and pitch-dark when we got back that night, to find our camp had moved—not a tent to be seen anywhere; so we all bivouacked where we could—such confusion, and such hunger! little or no food of any kind. I was generally pretty well off in this line, as I possessed a riding camel, on which my faithful *khitmutgar*, "Mr Bux," laden with some light provisions and the materials for making tea, used to follow me wherever I went; but on this occasion he was *non est*, and I was glad enough to get a portion of some cooked rations and a crust of bread from a sergeant of Highlanders, and then to a well-earned rest. The sepoys, though beaten and cowed as a body, showed many individual instances of valour. In truth, my own career was nearly cut short that day, by having got into difficulties with two or three of the enemy in a small tope of trees, when a gallant young Dogra sowar of "Hodson's

Horse," named "Beer-Bul," seeing I was hard pushed, came to my assistance and speedily killed two of my foes, leaving me only one to manage. For this act he received the Order of Valour. He rose to be a native officer in the 10th Bengal Lancers, one of the regiments raised from Hodson's Horse, and was later on transferred to the 12th Bengal Cavalry. He was with me in the Afghan campaign, and distinguished himself at the Peiwar Kotal,—subsequently, I regret to say, dying of cholera in the Kurrum valley.

On the following day a brigade under General Hope Grant started in pursuit of a considerable body of the rebels, who it was supposed had fled in the direction of Bithoor, the notorious Nana Sahib's estate. We marched twenty-four miles, and overtook them at a place called

Seraighat, on the banks of a river—where they were endeavouring to cross with their guns into Oude. After a smart encounter we took their guns, fifteen in number, with their baggage and everything they possessed, without having a man touched on our side. The majority of the enemy had escaped across the river, but many were drowned in the attempt. It was altogether a most complete little business, as we had now captured every gun the Gwalior Contingent had, and had dispersed their army, who had lost all they possessed. We had a good deal of difficulty in extricating the captured guns out of the shifting sand on the river-bank. Had we not caught them up just in time, I think the enemy would have had even a more difficult task in trying to convey them over the river.

We bivouacked that night on the banks.

What might have been a very unpleasant *fracas* occurred that evening. As our men were engaged in picketing their horses, and I was looking at my own, I heard in my camp unmistakable English or rather Irish oaths, and loud language, mixed with sounds of scuffling and equally high words in Punjabi from my men. I rushed to the spot, and found some soldiers of the 53rd Regiment — which was almost entirely composed of Irishmen, and, though a splendid fighting lot, rather out of hand at times—had chased a young bullock into our lines, and were in the act of slaughtering it: an act of the utmost sacrilege in the eyes of any Sikhs, and which, being about to be perpetrated in their very midst, roused their most fanatical religious feelings, which, needless to say, the hungry British soldiers did not understand, or, even if they did, would probably not have respected. I came up only just in time to save a terrible row—and perhaps bloodshed, for the Sikhs were almost beyond control, the native officers being as excited as themselves, and the comrades of the British soldiers were hurrying to the fray. It was with some difficulty I quelled the disturbance. It required considerable tact and management to appease and quiet both parties. The 53rd soldiers eventually retired to their own camp under their colonel's orders—and so the matter ended, to my great relief. It is curious how a little act of thoughtlessness or want of knowledge, reflecting on religious prejudices, will in a second fan into a flame feelings of bitter animosity.

The next day saw us at the Nana's palace of Bithoor, where we fondly hoped to line our pockets with loot and plunder; but, alas! our hopes were frustrated by the escape of the Nana, who got warning of our approach and fled with all his treasure. It was a fine palace, with lovely grounds; and in the peaceful times before the Mutiny was often the scene of gaiety and dissipation in the profusely hospitable entertainments which the Nana used to give to the European residents, civil and military, of Cawnpore. The furniture and fittings of the palace were speedily ransacked, broken up, and burnt by the soldiers.

A friend of mine in the Bengal Artillery came across some very singular correspondence, belonging to the Nana's chief counsellor and adviser, Azimoollah Khan. This man, whose birth and origin had been of the lowest, had, thanks to his natural cleverness, managed to worm himself into the Nana's most private confidence; and when his lord and master wished to send an emissary to England to appeal to the British Government against the Board of Directors for redress of his supposed wrongs, he found in Azimoollah a man just suited to the occasion. He was well educated in both English and French, had wonderful manners, was clever and unscrupulous. On his arrival in England, having good credentials and an unlimited command of money, he obtained admission to the best society in London and elsewhere—in fact, was lionised as freely as is still our fashion. He lived some two or three years in England, and when he returned to Bithoor was the Nana's right-hand man in all his entertainments.

The correspondence which was found showed Azimoollah to have been on the most intimate terms of friendship and freedom with many members of our highest aristocracy; and yet, on the Mutiny occurring, this very man proved himself to be a very fiend of fiends, and without exception the deadliest and most cruel enemy we had.

IV.

THE force under Sir Colin Campbell left Cawnpore on December 24th, moving up the Grand Trunk road; his object being to coerce the Nawab of Futteyghur (a rebel chief only second to the Nana in his treachery and atrocious murder of Europeans), and also to join hands with our second force from Delhi, as it was most essential the British should combine forces in their operations against Futteyghur, which was strongly held by the Nawab. The country through which we marched seemed to be returning to its normal state of quietude and subjection to British rule. *Thannahs* (police stations) were being established everywhere, and the telegraph set up again. I was much struck, one day's march out of Cawnpore, at coming across a *kafila* of Afghan traders, with their long string of camels, laden with dried fruits, boxes of grapes, skins, and the inevitable white Persian cat, moving quietly along the highroad on their way down to Calcutta—just as if nothing had ever occurred to disturb the peace of the country, or to endanger their traffic. No one had touched them or looted them, and they seemed to have no fears or dread of any such mishap, and I have no doubt they found their way down in safety and realised their usual gains and possibly more.

Whilst Sir Colin Campbell's force was

encamped at Meerun-Ka-Serai, on the Grand Trunk road, I was agreeably surprised by hearing that my commanding officer, Major Hodson—as he now was (having received his brevet majority for Delhi)—was in our camp, being the bearer of letters from General Seaton, whose column he had accompanied from Delhi, and which column was then, as well as I can recollect, encamped at Mynpoorie.

As a rule, any communications which passed between our force and that from Agra and Delhi were conveyed by highly-paid spies, who, with their lives in their hands, carried letters and despatches, not one-half of which probably reached their destination—owing to the death or treachery of the carriers. These letters were generally written in

French, Latin, or Greek, and, being wrapped in a quill or a small piece of hollow bamboo, were carried and concealed by the spies in the most marvellous manner — the relation of which would almost rival the fables of Munchausen. In order to obtain a personal communication, Hodson volunteered to ride through the enemy's forces occupying the Grand Trunk road, and convey despatches from General Seaton to the Commander-in-Chief, with but a small escort, consisting of one British officer, M'Dowall, and some twenty or twenty-five troopers. He made good his ride, but not without extreme danger and some loss, being discovered by the enemy's patrols, fired on, and pursued. This ride was a most gallant achievement, though only one of Hodson's many gallant deeds. It was a ride for life; and yet, when he reached the Chief's camp, he was as cool and calm as if he had only ridden from one brigade to another. This cool *insouciance* was one of Hodson's great characteristics: whether in the heat of action, or sitting at mess, he always seemed the same—nothing appeared to put him out (except on one very trying occasion, which I may describe hereafter). He had a wonderful knowledge and command of the native language, and was a thorough master of all the various idioms, phrases, and accents peculiar to the different districts through which we were campaigning; and by this knowledge, and his own keen commanding way of applying it, he was able to obtain the surest and best information. Sir Colin was much pleased at the result of his ride, and the opportunity of obtaining from such a reliable source the information he was so anxious to gain. Hodson rode back that same night to Seaton's camp, and accomplished his return journey, I believe, without incident. To my surprise, I learnt from him that my brother Charles had joined his regiment. I had thought he was still with the "Guides," but found that on the "Guides" returning to the Punjab after the siege of Delhi, my brother had volunteered to join "Hodson's Horse" on the march down country, and with them had served at the battles of Gungeree, Puttialee, &c.

On January 2nd, 1858, Sir Colin moved on with all his force to Futteyghur: on reaching the bridge over the Kala Nuddee river (about twelve miles from

Futteyghur) our passage was opposed by a large body of the enemy, who, with half a battery of artillery, had taken up a position behind a toll-house and embankment commanding the bridge.

As the head of our column came up our artillery speedily got into action, and soon silenced their guns. Though their infantry were still in position, the opposition was very slack, and certainly not enough to justify (as it seemed to us all) the long delay in the attack. The leading regiment of our column was the 53rd, commanded that day by Major Payn, afterwards General Sir William Payn, K.C.B., a very fine regiment, who, being mostly Irishmen, were eager to meet their enemy. Meanwhile I received orders to cross the river by a ford and get round the enemy's right flank; and had left for this purpose, and was crossing about a quarter of a mile lower down, when suddenly I heard loud cheering and a heavy musketry fire, and there I saw our troops gallantly advancing across the bridge to the assault. It turned out to be the 53rd, who, tired of the delay under fire, and, it was whispered, hearing that Sir Colin had sent for his pet Highlanders to take the bridge, took their bits between their teeth, and without any further orders determined to rush the bridge themselves—which they accordingly did, and with great success. The enemy, once forced out of their position, showed but a poor desultory fight, and, as at Cawnpore, fell an easy prey to the cavalry, who having crossed, some by the bridge, and others, including myself, by the ford, fell on them, and pursued them with such success that we captured every gun they had. I cannot easily forget the cheers the infantry, and especially the 53rd Regiment, gave us as we passed down the road to our camp after the pursuit. The 53rd were well pleased with themselves, and the result of the fight they had so suddenly initiated. But we heard that Sir Colin was greatly annoyed with them, and after the action rated them soundly for their insubordination. But little did these wild Irishmen care: they had had their fight, and a real good one, as far as they were concerned; and as Sir Colin concluded his speech of rebuke they gave him three cheers, and giving three cheers more for General Mansfield, Sir Colin's chief of the staff (who had formerly commanded their regiment), they quite upset the Chief's equanimity, but at the same time cleared away his wrath.

Poor Younghusband, commanding the squadron 5th Punjab Cavalry, was killed in this engagement. He had accompanied Watson, Probyn, and myself from Delhi, and was present in every engagement: we had almost looked on his as a charmed life after that episode of the well at Agra. A curious circumstance was connected with Younghusband's death. After the battle of Cawnpore he had purchased at auction a very smart helmet, which had been the property of Lieutenant Salmond, of the Gwalior Cavalry, who had been killed at Cawnpore. This helmet a good deal excited my envy and admiration, and as I had not possessed a decent head-dress since the Mutiny began, I had asked a friend to buy it for me at the auction of Salmond's effects. But poor Younghusband outbid me. At his sale I was again outbid, and the helmet fell to the nod of Lieutenant Havelock, a nephew of the General. He, too, was killed wearing it; and rumour subsequently said a fourth officer had bought it and had been killed. It was a strange coincidence, and as these deaths occurred quickly one after the other, I ceased to wish I had been its possessor.

After the action on the Kala Nuddee the fort and city of Futteyghur were occupied without further opposition, and a day or two afterwards Seaton's column joined the Commander-in-Chief's force, and with it the headquarters of Hodson's Horse, which I now rejoined after an absence of about three and a half months, reverting to my old position as adjutant. My commanding officer was much pleased with the appearance of the squadron after all their knocking about, and gave us considerable *kudos* for our maintenance of the good name of the regiment, accounts of which he he had heard from the Commander-in-Chief. He had been a little annoyed with me for not having kept him more fully acquainted with all we had been doing, and I had been slack in sending in the usual official information; but I often had not the means of so doing, and even in those days I fear I was not over-fond of "writing." However, any little feeling of anger on his part soon vanished in his pleasure at finding we had brought anything but discredit on "Hodson's Horse."

His words of praise tended much to console me in my regrets at the loss of my independent command, which had been such an eventful and responsible one. I was delighted to meet my brother and be in the same regiment with him. He was looking fit and well, and had seen lots of service both with the "Guides" round about Delhi and the neighbouring district, and also with Hodson on the march down. I was also very glad to meet my old Meerut chum, Charlie Sanford, who, commanding the "Guide" cavalry, had done excellent service at Delhi, and who was now appointed to command the squadron of the 5th Punjab Cavalry, vacant by Younghusband's death.

Contrary to my expectations, that when I resumed charge of the adjutant's office at headquarters, my short reign as commanding officer was over, to my great surprise I found myself detailed for another special duty; and as I was informed I had been selected by Sir Colin Campbell himself, I felt it to be a great honour. I was ordered to accompany Lieutenant John Watson of the 1st Punjab Cavalry, with a similar party (he being in command), on a secret service. As Watson was my senior, my selection was perhaps thereby accounted for. We started from Futteyghur on the night of January 13th, 1858, with "sealed orders," which were not to be opened till we reached a certain point. On arrival there we found our duty was to proceed to Meerun-Ka-Serai, on the Cawnpore road, about the junction of the road from Futteyghur to Cawnpore and the Grand Trunk road from Calcutta to Delhi; and there to watch the roads and the fords of the river Ganges lying between Oude and the North-Western Province. It was generally believed that the Nana would attempt to escape from Oude, now in the full occupation of the enemy, and make his way to Central India. At Meerun-Ka-Serai we found a regiment of Punjab infantry under the command of Major "Jack" Stafford, a fine big man and a good soldier, and a most amusing and entertaining companion. His regiment had established a capital mess, and having made us all honorary members, we fed sumptuously every day and had a right good time of it. There was plenty of sport about, both shooting and pig-sticking, and we had tent-pegging (then a comparatively new accomplishment) and other sports.

But no Nana or other invader came near us, and we began to think our services were being thrown away. I managed, however, to have one little excitement, which I half hoped might be the making of me. I was in charge of the camp. Watson, Stafford, and I think every other officer excepting young Anderson of the 1st Punjab Cavalry, had gone out shooting or pig-sticking, when a native letter was put into my hand, the messenger telling me it was *bahut zaroorat*, or "very urgent," and the contents of which I mastered with much difficulty. It turned out to be a note from the tehsildar of Nana Mhow Ghat, a landing-place and ford on the river, begging for immediate assistance, as the Nana, he said, was crossing the river. Naturally Anderson and I were much excited, and we promptly got together some eighty or ninety sowars and started for the Ghat, twenty miles, at a round trot, full of the hope that we were going to catch the Nana, and picturing to ourselves the receipt of the Government reward, to say nothing of the *éclat* that would be ours!

On arrival at the village the tehsildar met us, and assured us the enemy were about to cross; and certainly we did see some boat-loads of sepoys on the other side of the river, but it very soon turned out that they had received intelligence of our movements, and were on their return to their own shore. Whether the Nana was of the party or not, it is difficult to say. The tehsildar, however, declared his intelligence was correct, and that the arch-scoundrel was there. We had a hot and dusty ride for nothing; but we remained there that night, sleeping on the banks of the river in hopes of a further attempt on their part, and our only consolation was the arrival of John Watson, who, the instant he heard we had started on our excursion, came after us as fast as he could with another detachment, only to be equally sold! The arrival of companions in our disappointment was curiously soothing to our feelings. We returned to our camp next day, where we had but little to do: everything was perfectly quiet, and with the exception of people travelling up and down country we saw no one. A convoy of ladies and officers arrived on their way home—amongst them Brigadier Greathed on his way to join his appointment in Bombay. I was sorry he was leaving us: he had always been a kind friend to me.

Thus it will be seen that our time at Meerun-Ka-Serai was not a very profitable one in the way of fighting: on the contrary, to me it was a great loss, as I thereby missed being in for a good thing. I suddenly got an order to return to regimental headquarters with my detachment, and of course lost no time in doing so, as Hodson had given me a hint there might be some fighting. Alas! on reaching Futteyghur I found the fight was over. "Hodson's Horse" had accompanied a force under General Hope Grant against a strong body of the rebels, and, coming across them at Shumshabad, had inflicted on them a good thrashing. And my regiment came in for some very smart fighting, but with some sad results —in the death of Charlie M'Dowall, our second in command, who was killed by almost the first round-shot fired by the enemy, and in Hodson himself being severely wounded twice by sabre-cuts on his arm. My brother, I heard, had two narrow escapes—one from a spent bullet which a rebel sowar had fired point-blank at him; the other from a spear-wound, which a man was in the act of delivering when Hodson came up and disposed of his adversary. Altogether they appeared to have had a very rough *mêlée*, and I was much disappointed in being just too late. After this affair of Shumshabad, Sir Colin, having detached a force to operate against the Rohilkund rebels, proceeded with his main body towards Lucknow, *viâ* Cawnpore, for the final capture of that city.

We ("Hodson's Horse") reached Cawnpore early in February, and, pushing on beyond that place, were encamped for some little time at Oonao, one march or so on the Lucknow side of the river. Sir Colin in the meanwhile was massing his army, and distributing it into divisions and brigades.

During our stay at Oonao my time was fully occupied with outpost duty, convoys, &c., and drilling the men, for they were still very raw at any form of discipline or manœuvrings, and, time being short, the process of instruction was rather "forcible" than "persuasive"; but they were keen, if a little stupid, and I think rather liked that form of lesson than otherwise.

One day I was sent in from there to Cawnpore to bring out arrears of pay for the regiment, and on this occasion I made my first acquaintance with Colonel

Robert Napier, Bengal Engineers (to whom Hodson had given me a letter of introduction), afterwards so well known as Field-Marshal Lord Napier of Magdâla, who received me with the kindness he never failed to show to me in all the years I knew him and served under him in after-life—a great and famous soldier, whom it was a privilege to know. He was one of Hodson's greatest friends, and I have always considered this fact a strong proof of Hodson's acquittal of the serious charges brought against him. Napier would never have admitted an unworthy man to his friendship.

On February 24th, 1858, we received an order to make a forced march to the Alum Bagh to reinforce Outram, who was threatened by a large body of rebels. Outram had held the Alum Bagh ever since our relief of and retirement from Lucknow in November. He had had a good deal of fighting on and off, but had well maintained his position.

We marched all that night, and arrived at Alum Bagh on the early morning of the 25th (our light baggage had come up with us), when we received orders to be ready to turn out at a moment's notice. We had just time to have an early tea and a poached egg or two, which, after the long night's march, was most acceptable; and I was contemplating a change from my dirty old cord breeches into a brand-new pair just received from Calcutta, when a curious sort of presentiment that I should probably spoil the latter that day made me decide in favour of the old unmentionable garment: but before I had leisure to waver in my prudent resolve, the order came to "Turn out." A large body of rebels had come up during the night to threaten our flank. It did not take us long to mount and be off.

This was my first day in action with "Hodson's Horse" as a complete regiment, for when at the siege of Delhi the corps was in its infancy, and when I left Delhi with my wing it was certainly not weaned; but now we were a full-blown regiment, men better equipped, clothed, and drilled, and the horses of a better stamp, and with decent saddlery and accoutrements. When I say a regiment, I might almost call it a brigade, for by Hodson's influence and the magic power of his name recruits from the Punjab had come flocking in, and I should say we were nearly a thousand strong. We were complete in officers, and altogether made a brave show as we advanced to our work.

No time was to be lost, as the enemy had already heard of the reinforcements which had come in during the night, and were in full retreat to Lucknow. Our camp was not far from the Alum Bagh, and our route to meet the enemy lay by the village of Jellalabad, passing close by the scene of my previous encounter with them at the relief of Lucknow: in fact, we passed so close that I was able, *en passant*, to give Hodson a hurried description of the fight. When we now came in view of the enemy, they were passing in rather a disorganised mass right across our front as we advanced. We could see they had a couple of field-guns, one gun being about six hundred yards ahead of the other. The main body was almost entirely infantry, and all were mutineers, arrayed in uniform. Our rapid approach had a great effect upon them: they seemed to make no effort to rally and stand, and, as we advanced and charged, we got well into them, and the whole affair seemed over. The rearmost gun was in our possession, and the enemy, as far as we had encountered them, in full flight; but somehow, owing to the ardour of the charge and the pursuit, our regiment got quite out of hand, lost all formation, and scattered; and they, seeing our condition, and probably having a leader with a good cool head, rallied round their remaining gun, regained their formation as we lost ours, and, pouring in volleys of musketry with discharges of grape from their gun, rendered our confusion worse confounded. Our men, gallant and forward in pursuit or a charge, could not stand being hammered at a disadvantage: there was a din of shouting and noise, officers doing their best to bring the men up, but all to no effect; and it looked sadly probable that "Hodson's Horse" would in their turn retreat. Hodson at this crisis managed to get a few brave spirits together—not more than a dozen. Well I remember him, with his arm in a sling from his wound at Shumshabad, shouting to the men to follow him as he made an attempt to charge. He and I were riding close together, and as we advanced with our small following, I saw his horse come down with him; and the next instant my own charger, my beloved "Tearaway," reared straight up and fell dead. The fire was most deadly: the range was short, and just suited to the point-blank fire from the smooth-bore musket under which we were exposed, so that nearly every one of our small party was killed or wounded. Fortunately I fell clear of my horse, and catching a sowar's whose rider had just been killed, I speedily mounted, and, as good luck would have it, was able to rally our men to a certain extent, who, seeing our supports coming up (7th Hussars and Military Train), now came on with a will, and, charging the remaining gun, scattered the enemy in all directions. My temporary charger—a small grey country-bred mare—carried me well, and we followed the enemy in pursuit, the British cavalry also cutting in. It was no easy matter, as they (the enemy) had got amongst trees and low jungle, and were guarded by a village where cavalry were not of much use. In the ardour of pursuit I had got ahead of my men, when I came upon a couple of sepoys on their way to the village. They had their bayonets fixed, and seeing me unsupported, stood—one in my direct front and the other on my right. I made for the former; but the one on the right took aim at me as I passed and shot me clean through the thigh, the bullet going through my saddle and my horse, killing her dead. Fortunately I fell clear, though helpless. My opponent was just coming up to finish me off, when he was sabred by a trooper of the Military Train.

The affair was now over; the enemy suffered severely and were driven back into Lucknow, and we returned to camp, and I was much pleased to think that our men had retrieved their previous discomfiture. Their temporary "funk" was really due to their having got out of hand after their first charge, and not having time to rally before they had again to face the enemy's heavy musketry fire. The steadiest cavalry in the world might have found it difficult, and to an absolutely newly-raised regiment the position was a very trying one.

Hodson had been unable to remount after his horse was shot, so I had the honour of leading the final charge—for which he gave me much credit; but he was greatly annoyed at the behaviour of the men, and especially the native officers, and taking some of them round to my *dooly* when I was being carried back to camp, accused them of being the cause of my being shot: but I gladly forgave them all, for they were really gallant fellows, and had shown their good qualities on many a former occasion. There was one native officer, though, a smart-looking young Afghan, who had been Hodson's especial pet, he having been his orderly when he commanded the "Guides," who certainly showed the white feather most unmistakably. When we were trying to rally the men, Hodson called on him by name ("Nuzrut Jung") to follow him, but he slunk back into the crowd, and did not show up again till it was over, when he came to make his salaams and we refused to speak to him. I saw this man in Kabul many years after, he having retired to his own country on a pension;

and though he professed to be a friend to the British Government, I could never trust him, and I believe there were strong suspicions that he was then a traitor as well as a coward.

The death of my favourite charger "Tearaway," Phillip's legacy, was a sad blow to me—he had carried me so gallantly through all my work and fighting. It was another friend gone.

My wound, of course, placed me *hors de combat*, as far as any further fighting took place, for some time; but I remained in camp with my regiment, being well attended to by our doctor, Anderson, a very capable, kindly man. During the previous ten days or so my brother had been detached with a squadron to accompany a force under General Hope Grant, and had come in for a very good thing at the action of "Meangunge," in Oude, where he distinguished himself greatly, especially by saving the life of Major Anson of the 9th Lancers, for which act, in addition to his previous act of gallantry in saving my life at Khurkhouda, already described, he subsequently received the Victoria Cross. He rejoined the regiment some few days after I was wounded.

During the first part of the siege of Lucknow, "Hodson's Horse" was encamped between the Alum Bagh and the Dilkoosha, their duty consisting of watching the country all about, and making reconnaissances.

I lay on my bed in camp, feeling sick and disgusted at being left inactive and disabled—though I believe I did not lose much, for the cavalry work was not very brilliant or lively, all the heavy fighting falling on the artillery and infantry. However, I made a rapid recovery, and ere very long could limp about on crutches.

The wound had been a very clean one, and the shot fired so close that it had scorched my breeches (I congratulated myself I had not worn my brand-new ones!)—the bullet carrying the torn cloth right through my leg. Seeing me getting on so well, Hodson, who also was unable to ride, was one day driving into Lucknow, and asked me to accompany him. I tried, but was unable to get up into the dog-cart, and so he started by himself. He nodded a cheerful "good-bye" to me as he drove off with his orderly, "Nihal Singh." Little did I think at the moment I should never see him again! Had I been able to accompany him, it is possible events might have turned out otherwise; he would probably have remained to look after me, and thus avoided his fate: as it was, he drove into the headquarters camp, saw his friends, did what business there was to do, and I believe was actually in his trap to return when he heard the sound of the attack on the Kaiser Bagh, and, naturally enough for a man of his soldierly and fighting temperament, returned to join in the fight or see the result. He was mortally wounded, was brought back to the headquarters camp, and died some hours afterwards. A finer or more gallant soldier never breathed. He had the true instincts of a leader of men; as a cavalry soldier he was perfection, a strong seat on horseback (though an ugly rider), a perfect swordsman, nerves like iron, and with a quick, intelligent eye, indefatigable and zealous, and with great tact. He had the all-round qualities of a good soldier. Great was the grief in "Hodson's Horse" at the death of their leader, for no man was more loved by his men. To me his death was a sad loss—he had been a kind friend to me from the day I joined him at Delhi. I had been longer with him than any of the surviving officers, and I knew him better than most.

Another sorrow came to me about the same time in the death of my brother-officer and chum, Charlie Sanford. He was killed while gallantly scaling the wall of a house when scouting through a village, by a shot from an unseen enemy. Only a few days before he had come to see me and reproached me for my foolhardiness, and yet fell a victim to his own recklessness. A curious incident was told me after his death: on the receipt of the news that he had been gazetted to a brevet majority for his services at Delhi when commanding the "Guide" cavalry, his brother-officers drank his health at mess. In his speech in reply he said he had a presentiment he should not live to enjoy his newly won honours,—that he was convinced he would be shot, but not in a cavalry charge or fair fight. Poor fellow! the next day realised his sad forebodings.

After Hodson's death the regiment was ordered to join the Cavalry Division, and they took part in the fruitless endeavour to cut off the retreat of the mutineers from Lucknow. I was taken into hospital at the Dilkoosha, and on March 25th, just a month after I was wounded, I started with a convoy for Cawnpore *en route* to the hills, where I was sent on nine months' leave. With this I severed my connection with "Hodson's Horse," having served in many exciting events with that regiment. I had been its first adjutant when Hodson, M'Dowall, and myself were its only three officers. They were both gone, and I was invalided and unfit for duty, and my place was filled up. Though its distinguished commandant was dead, the regiment continued to maintain its reputation under his successor—Colonel Daly (afterwards Sir Henry Daly, G.C.B.); did gallant service during the remainder of the Mutiny; was subsequently made into three regiments—1st, 2nd, and 3rd

"Hodson's Horse"; and finally, on the reorganisation of the native army, the 1st and 2nd regiments were renumbered and renamed 9th and 10th Bengal Lancers (both these regiments retaining the additional title of "Hodson's Horse"), whilst the 3rd regiment was disbanded. I do not wish to be invidious, but I have no hesitation in saying that the 9th and 10th (Duke of Cambridge's Own) Bengal Lancers are quite among the pick of the Bengal cavalry of the present day—in each case mainly due to the Sikh and Punjabi element they possess, the result of Hodson's great name and reputation amongst the natives of the Punjab, whereby he secured the best and most warlike men to his standard.

It took me some months to fully

recover the effects of my wound. During this interval I received the happy intelligence of my having been gazetted to the Victoria Cross. A subsequent 'Gazette' brought my brother the same glad news for himself. Towards the end of my leave, when a medical board pronounced me fit for active service again, I was offered the appointment of second in command of the 2nd Mahratta Horse, about to be raised by Major F. H. Smith, a well-known Irregular Cavalry officer. The Mahratta cavalry had in former days acquired a great reputation in the native armies of Central India, and it was thought possible we might be successful in renewing it in the British service; but the recruits we enlisted turned out a great failure. Major Smith then proceeded to raise the regiment at

Meerut and Bolundshuhur, recruiting "Jats" only — a race of agriculturists descended from a warlike tribe who had formerly conquered that country. They were fine, manly-looking fellows, but were very dull and wanting in natural smartness and quickness. However, after we had collected about a hundred or a hundred and fifty sabres, we were ordered to proceed to Morar, Gwalior, the capital of the Mahratta country, with a view to completing our complement with the natives of that country. Whilst on our march to Morar, Major Smith and I, being the only two officers with the newly-raised squadron, took the opportunity of trying to teach our raw recruits some minor elements of drill, which with the dunderheaded Jat ploughman was not so easy or natural a task as with the more warlike Sikh. We arrived at our destination just in time to take a share in Sir Robert Napier's dashing pursuit of the Delhi royal prince, Feroze Shah, ending with the action and complete dispersal of his followers at Ranode.

About a day or two before our arrival at Morar, Sir Robert Napier had received intelligence that Feroze Shah, with a following of about two thousand rebels, was endeavouring to make his way across Bundelkund towards Central India, hoping to join forces with the famous Tantia Topee, then—and indeed all throughout—about the most energetic and restless of the rebel leaders. Sir Robert determined to try and cut off Feroze Shah before he could effect this union; and with this object he organised a movable column, consisting of a squadron of the 14th Light Dragoons, about a hundred of the 71st Highland Light Infantry (as a camel corps), and to our great delight he included our newly arrived cavalry in his column. He had also with him a small body of independent Punjab cavalry (then called the Towanna Horse), under a native leader named Jehan Khan. With this small but very mobile force Napier left Morar on, I think, December 13th, 1858, starting down the Jhansi road. Finding after the first march that the enemy had eluded him, but gathering from his information that they were not long ahead of him, he gave immediate chase. And a fine chase it was; for the enemy had entered into the jungles, and, lightly equipped as they were and mostly mounted on ponies, without any baggage or impedimenta, were not easy to catch. Fortunately we were also lightly equipped, and were promptly on the trail, as, like themselves, we had no impedimenta and no dismounted men. For two days and three nights, as far as my recollection carries me, we followed up our friends, guided by their tracks and smouldering camp-fires (of local information there was but little, as the whole country was a thick jungle), until at last, on the early morning of December 17th, we were absolutely so close on them (as we thought) that we came across some of their stragglers. Peter Lumsden, Assistant Quartermaster-General to the force, was riding on ahead of the column, and in the early morning dawn saw two men on horseback riding alongside of him, their heads and bodies being enveloped in long cloaks to keep off the cold. Thinking they were two of our Towanna Horse, he took no notice of them; but he soon found out his mistake, as at the first sight of a European face the men had slipped off their ponies and in an instant were hidden in the jungle. This meeting raised our hopes high; but not long after, as daylight broke, the column emerged from the jungle on to a fair-sized plateau, and from that moment we lost sight and scent of our quarry. Pathways and tracks led in various directions, but not a sign of our enemy. Our disappointment was great. Lumsden now suggested we should make for the village of Ranode, some three or four miles off, to see if we could there gain any information; and so it was settled, and off we went. On arriving near the village (a considerable-sized one) we found the inhabitants all turned out, lining the walls as if for defence. After some parleying we found that the villagers had mistaken us for Feroze Shah's force; as he had sent them word of his approach, with orders to produce supplies, &c., and they were prepared to resist. This was good news for us, as it was further reported that in a certain time our mutual enemy would appear.

Our little force, which, all told, did not, I fancy, amount to more than three hundred and fifty, were carefully disposed in ambush, and we awaited the course of events.

We had not long to wait, for we had

scarcely got ourselves into position when in the distance was to be seen the dust and commotion of a considerable body of men approaching. They must have taken a circuitous route, after having, as they imagined, given us the slip, and were now advancing on Ranode, which they intended to requisition for supplies. The General allowed them to advance until they were well in our front, and no longer being in a jungle, but on an open plain, were thoroughly exposed to our attack, when the order was given to us to "Advance and charge." We were down on them like lightning, and in an instant all was confusion, slaughter, and flight. Feroze Shah was the first to bolt, and being splendidly mounted, to our deep regret got away, but of the rest their leaders were mostly killed: beyond occasional single combats or men fighting in despair no resistance was made. It was a case of *sauve qui peut* from start to finish. Our newly-raised recruits were not in it with the 14th Light Dragoons, who rode like mad; so finding my men could not go the pace, I attached myself to a troop of the 14th, and for seven miles over a most break-neck country, black cotton soil with cracks and fissures large enough to swallow a camel, did we pursue! I was riding a well-known Arab racehorse, "The Master of Elibank," which I had purchased some few months before, and he carried me like a bird—though as I galloped along on this awful ground I could not help casting an occasional wish that we might come safely out of it. It is difficult to say what our total was that day, but we cut up numbers, and dispersed the whole gathering, besides capturing some six or seven elephants, returning with minds much at ease after our long and arduous pursuit. Our own casualties were happily very small — Captain Prettejohn of the 14th got a severe sabre-cut across the thigh. On my way back I passed him, much distressed, not at being wounded, but at being unable to get at his cigars, which, being in his holster, had disappeared with his horse!

Sir Robert Napier was much pleased at having brought his long chase to such a satisfactory close, and he frequently in after-days alluded to it with pleasure.

This forced march gave me my first experience of a Camel Corps on service, and their great advantages impressed me much: each camel should carry two soldiers, but the men of the 71st not being experienced in the art of driving camels, there was on this occasion only one British soldier to each beast, with a native driver. The 71st were sturdy thick-set men, rather short in the leg; and as neither riding nor driving was much in their line, were a little troubled by the uneasy motion of their mount: some of their expressions were very comical. As a rule, the Camel Corps marched just in advance of our men, and as the lazy beasts were wont to lag, my commanding officer once suggested to the rearmost Highlander that he should trot on. His reply was, "And hoo can I trot with my skeen sae sair?"—a most unanswerable rejoinder.

After the action of Ranode our force

marched for a time about the jungles in pursuit of Tantia Topee, pulling up at Goonah and Augur, then the head-quarters of Meade's Horse, a regiment which did very good service, Major Meade himself eventually capturing the renowned Tantia.

We subsequently returned to Morar; and with this expedition under Sir Robert Napier ended my services in the Indian Mutiny.